CHRONICLES OF CANADA

Edited by George M. Wrong and H. H. Langton

In thirty-two volumes

31

ALL AFLOAT

BY WILLIAM WOOD

Part IX

National Highways

THE VOYAGEURS ON A MISTY MORNING

From a painting by Verner

ALL AFLOAT

A Chronicle of Craft and Waterways

BY

WILLIAM WOOD

TORONTO
GLASGOW, BROOK & COMPANY
1915

*Copyright in all Countries subscribing to
the Berne Convention*

TO
THE PETRYS
EACH AND ALL
IN TOKEN OF
A FAMILY FRIENDSHIP
FOUR GENERATIONS STRONG

CONTENTS

ILLUSTRATIONS

CHAPTER I

A LAND OF WATERWAYS

CANADA is the child of the sea. Her infancy was cradled by her waterways; and the life-blood of her youth was drawn from oceans, lakes, and rivers. No other land of equal area has ever been so intimately bound up with the changing fortunes of all its different waters, coast and inland, salt and fresh.

The St Lawrence basin by itself is a thing to marvel at, for its mere stupendous size alone. Its mouth and estuary are both so vast that their salt waters far exceed those of all other river systems put together. Its tide runs farther in from the Atlantic than any other tide from this or any other ocean. And its 'Great Lakes' are appropriately known by their proud name because they contain more fresh water than all the world beside. Size for size, this one river system is so pre-eminently first in the sum of these three attributes that there is no competing second to be found elsewhere.

It forms a class of its own. And well it may, even for its minor attributes, when the island of Newfoundland at its mouth exceeds the area of Ireland ; when the rest of its mouth could contain Great Britain ; when an arm of the true deep sea runs from Cabot Strait five hundred miles inland to where the Saguenay river soundings go down beyond an average of a hundred fathoms; and when, three hundred miles farther inland still, on an island in an archipelago at the mouth of the Ottawa, another tributary stream, there stands the city of Montreal, one of the greatest seaports in the world.

But mere size is not the first consideration. The Laurentian waters are much more important for their significance in every stage of national development. They were the highway to the heart of America long before the white man came. They remained the same great highway from Cartier to Confederation— a period of more than three hundred years. It is only half a century since any serious competition by road and rail began. Even now, in spite of this competition, they are one of the greatest of all highways. Nor does their significance stop here. Nature laid out the St Lawrence basin so that it not only led into the heart of the continent, but connected with every other system from the Atlantic to the Pacific and from the Tropics to the Polar sea. Little by little the pioneers found out that they could paddle and portage the same canoe, by inland routes, many thousands of miles to all four points of the compass : eastward to the Atlantic between the Bay of Fundy and New York ; westward till, by extraordinary efforts, they passed up the giant Saskatchewan and through the mighty ranges that look on the Pacific ; southward to the Mississippi and the Gulf of Mexico ; northward to Hudson Bay, or down the Mackenzie to the Arctic ocean.

As settlement went on and Canada developed westwards along this unrivalled waterway man tried to complete for his civilized wants what nature had so well provided for his savage needs. There is a rise of six hundred feet between Lake St Peter and Lake Superior. So canals were begun early in the nineteenth century and gradually built farther and farther west, at a total cost of $125,000,000, till, by the end of the century, with the opening of the Canadian ' Soo,' the last artificial link was finished and direct navigation was established between the western end of Lake

Superior at Duluth and the eastern end of the
St Lawrence system at Belle Isle, a distance of
no less than 2340 miles.

But even the mighty St Lawrence, with the
far-reaching network of its connecting systems,
is not the whole of Canada's waters. The
eastern coast of Nova Scotia is washed by the
Atlantic, and the whole length of British
Columbia by the Pacific. Then, there are
harbours, fiords, lakes, and navigable rivers not
directly connected with either of these coasts
or with the wonderfully ramified St Lawrence.
So, taking every factor of size and significance
into consideration, it seems almost impossible
to exaggerate the magnitude of the influence
which waterways have always exerted, and are
still exerting, on the destinies of Canada.

Canada touches only one country by land.
She is separated from every other foreign
country and joined to every other part of the
British Empire by the sea alone. Her land
frontier is long and has given cause for much
dispute in times of crisis. But her water
frontiers—her river, lake, and ocean frontiers—
have exercised diplomacy and threatened complications with almost constant persistence
from the first. There were conflicting rights,
claims, and jurisdictions about the waters long

before the Dominion was ever thought of. Discovery, exploration, pioneering, trade, and fisheries, all originated questions which, involving mercantile sea-power, ultimately turned on naval sea-power and were settled by the sword. Each rival was forced to hold his own at sea or give up the contest. Even in time of peace there was incessant friction along the many troublous frontiers of the sea. From the Treaty of Utrecht in 1713 down to the final award at The Hague, nearly two centuries later, the diplomatic war went steadily on. It is true that the fishing grounds of Newfoundland were the chief object of contention. But Canada and Newfoundland are so closely connected by geographical, imperial, and maritime bonds that no just account of craft and waterways can be given if any attempt is made to separate such complementary parts of British North America. They will therefore be treated as one throughout the present book.

But, even apart from Newfoundland, the Canadian interests concerned rather with the water than the land make a most remarkable total. They include questions of international waterways and water-power, salt and fresh water fishing, sealing, whaling, inland navigation, naval armaments on the Great Lakes, canals, drainage, and many more. The British ambassador who left Washington in 1913 declared officially that most of his attention had been devoted to Canadian affairs ; and most of these Canadian affairs were connected with the water. Nor was there anything new in this, or in its implication that Canadian waters brought Canada into touch with international questions, whether she wished it or not. The French shore of Newfoundland; the *Alabama* claims ; the San Juan boundary ; the whole purport of the Treaty of Washington in 1871 ; the *Trent* affair of ten years earlier; the Panama Canal tolls of to-day ; the War of 1812 ; the war which others called the Seven Years' War, but which contemporary England called the ' Maritime War ' ; all the invasions of Canada, all the trade with the Indians, all Spanish, French, Dutch, British, and American complications — everything, in fact, which helped to shape Canadian destinies—were inevitably connected with the sea ; and, more often than not, were considered and settled mainly as a part of what those prescient pioneers of oversea dominion, the great Elizabethan statesmen, always used to call ' the sea affair.'

Canada, like other countries, may be looked at from many points of view ; but there is none that does not somehow include her oceans, lakes, or rivers. Her waterways, of course, are only one factor in her history. But they are a constant factor, everywhere at work, though sometimes little recognized, and making their influence felt throughout the length and breadth of the land. If any one would see what the water really means to Canada, let him compare her history with Russia's. Russia and Canada are both northern countries and both continental, with many similarities in natural resources. But their extremely different forms of government are not so unlike each other as are their differing relations with the sea. The unlikeness of the two peoples accounts for a good deal ; but this only emphasizes the maritime character of Canada. Russia is essentially an empire of the land. Canada is the greatest link between the oceans which unite the Empire of the Sea.

Take any aspect of sea-power, naval or mercantile, and British interest in it is at once apparent. Take the mere statistics of tonnage —tonnage built, tonnage afloat, tonnage armed. The British Navy has over a third of the world's effective naval tonnage ; the British Empire has nearly half of the whole world's mercantile marine; and the United Kingdom alone builds more than three-fifths of the world's new tonnage every year. When all the other elements of sea-power are taken into consideration—the people who are directly dependent on the sea, the values constantly afloat, the credits involved, the enormous advantages enjoyed, and the clinching fact that British naval defeat means disaster and disaster means ruin—when all this is brought into the reckoning, it is safe to say that the combined maritime interests of the British Empire practically equal those of all the rest of the world put together. When it is also remembered that Canada, itself a land of waterways, contains a third of the total area of the Empire, and lies between the Atlantic and Pacific oceans, the significance of these facts is placed beyond a doubt.

Take a very different illustration—the speech of Canada to-day—and the significance is still the same. We have so many sea terms in our ordinary English speech that we almost forget that they are sea terms at all till we compare them with corresponding idioms in other languages. Then we realize that only the Dutch, the Finns, and the Scandinavians can

approach the English-speaking peoples in the
common use of sea terms. Other foreigners
employ different phrasing altogether. Their
landsmen never ' clear the decks for action,'
are never ' brought up with a round turn,' or
even ' taken aback,' as if by the wind on the
wrong side. They never have ' three sheets
in the wind,' even when they do get ' half seas
over.' They don't ' throw a man overboard,'
even when the man is one of those unfortunates
who is apt to get ' on his beam ends.' The
facetious ' don't speak to the man at the
wheel ' and the cautious ' you 'd better not sail
so close to the wind ' have no exact equivalents
for the Slav or Latin man in the street.

These, and many more, are common ex-
pressions which Anglo-Canadians share with
the stay-at-home type of Englishman. But
the special point is that, like the American, the
Canadian is still more nautical than the
Englishman in his everyday use of sea terms.
' So long ! ' in the sense of good-bye is a
seaport valediction commoner in Canada
than in England. Canadians go ' timber-cruising ' when they are looking for merchantable
trees ; they used to understand what ' prairie
schooners ' were out West ; and even now
they always ' board ' a train wherever it may

be. But even more remarkable are the sea terms universally current among the French Canadians, who come from the seafaring branch of a race of landsmen. Under the French régime the army officers used to say they felt as if they were on board a man-of-war as long as they stayed in Canada. The modern Parisian may think the same to-day when he is told how to steer his way about the country roads by the points of the compass. The word *lanierne* is unknown, for the nautical *fanal* invariably takes its place. The winter roads are marked out by 'buoys' (*balises*), and if you miss the 'channel' between them you may 'founder' (*caler*) and then become a 'derelict' (completely *dégradé*). You must *embarquer* into a carriage and *débarquer* out of it. A cart is *radou'ée*, as if repaired in a dockyard. Even a well-dressed woman is said to be *bi'n gré-yée*, that is, she is 'fit to go foreign.' Horses are not tied but moored (*amarrés*); enemies are reconciled by being re-moored (*ramarrés*); and the Quebec winter is supposed to begin with a 'broadside' of snow on November 25 (*la bordée de la Sainte-Catherine*).

No wonder Canadian French and English speech is full of sea terms. Even when the

Canadians themselves forget, as they are very apt to do, the indispensable naval side of sea-power, they can account for most kinds of nauticality by their economic history, which all depended, directly or indirectly, down to the smallest detail, on the mercantile marine—especially if we give the name of mercantile marine its justifiable extension so as to cover all the craft that ply on inland waterways as well as those that cross the sea. It is calculated at the present day that it is as easy to move a hundred tons by water as ten tons by rail or one ton by road; and this rule, in spite of many local exceptions, is fairly correct in practice, especially as distances increase. Now, Canada is a country of great distances; and by land she once was in nearly every part, and she still is in a few parts, a country of obstructive wilds. What, then, must have been the advantage of water carriage over land carriage when there was neither road nor rail? As even pack-horses were not available in the early days, and good roads were few and only established by very slow degrees, it is well within the mark to say that the sum-total of advantage in favour of water over land carriage, up to a time which old men can remember, must have been at least a thousand to one.

It would be natural to suppose that some knowledge of the sea was widely diffused among the British peoples in general and Canadians in particular. But this is far from being the case. Though there is three times as much sea as land in the world, it is safe to say that there is three hundred times as much knowledge of the land as there is of the sea. The ways of the sea are strange to most people in every country, excepting Norway and Newfoundland. Seamen have always been somewhat of a class apart, though they are less so now. Ignorance of everything to do with the water is exceedingly common, even in England and Canada. The British mercantile marine is one of the biggest commercial enterprises of all time. It is of very great importance to Canada. It is absolutely vital to England. Yet it is less understood among the general public than any other kind of business that is of national concern. Some people even think that the mercantile marine differs from every other kind of business in being under the special care of the government. They are probably misled by the term ' Merchant Service,' which, when spelt with capital letters, has a very official look and reminds them of the two great fighting ' services,' the Army and the Navy. In reality

THE SPIRIT OF THE LAKES
By Lorado Taft, in the Chicago Art Institute

the merchant service is no more a government
service than any other kind of trade is.

Ignorance about the Navy is commoner still.
Canadian history is full of sea-power, but
Canadian histories are not. It was only in
1909, a hundred and fifty years after the Battle
of the Plains, that the first attempt was made
to introduce the actual naval evidence into the
story of the Conquest by publishing a selection
from the more than thirty thousand daily
entries made in the logs of the men-of-war
engaged in the three campaigns of Louisbourg,
Quebec, and Montreal. Yet there were twice
as many sailors under Saunders as there were
soldiers under Wolfe, and the fleet that
carried them was the greatest single fleet which,
up to that time, had ever appeared in any
waters. How many people, even among
Canadians born and bred, know that there have
already been two local Canadian navies of
different kinds and two Canadian branches of
Imperial navies oversea ; that in 1697 a naval
battle was fought in the waters of Hudson Bay,
opposite Port Nelson ; that seigneurial grants
during the French régime made reservations of
man-of-war oak for the service of the crown ;
that while Bougainville, the famous French
circumnavigator, was trying to keep Wolfe

out of Quebec, Captain Cook, the famous British circumnavigator, was trying to help him in ; that there was steamer transport in the War of 1812 ; that the first steam man-of-war to fire a shot in action was launched on the St Lawrence four years before the first railway in Canada was working ; that just before Confederation more than half the citizens of the ancient capital were directly dependent on ship-building and nearly all the rest on shipping ; and that the Canadian fisheries of the present day are the most important in the world ? As a matter of fact, there are very few Canadians or other students of Canadian history who fully realize what Canada owes to the sea. How many know that her ' sea affairs ' may have begun a thousand years ago, if the Norsemen came by way of Greenland ; that she has a long and varied naval history, with plenty of local privateering by the way ; that the biggest sail-ing vessel to make a Scottish port in the heyday of the clippers was Canadian-built all through ; that Canada built another famous vessel for a ruling prince in India ; that most Arctic ex-ploration has been done in what are properly her waters ; that she was the pioneer in ocean navigation entirely under steam ; and that she is now beginning to revive, with steam and steel, the shipbuilding industry with which she did so much in the days of mast and sail and wooden hulls ?

No exhaustive Canadian 'water history' can possibly be attempted here. That would require a series of its own. But at least a first attempt will now be made to give some general idea of what such a history would contain in fuller detail : of the kayaks and canoes the Eskimos and Indians used before the white man came, and use to-day, in the ever-receding wilds ; of the various small craft moved by oar and sail that slowly displaced the craft moved only by the paddle ; of the sailing vessels proper, and how they plied along Canadian waterways, and out beyond, on all the Seven Seas ; of the steamers, which, in their earlier pioneering days, shed so much forgotten lustre on Canadian enterprise ; of those ' Codlands of North America ' and other teeming fisheries which the far-seeing Lord Bacon rightly thought ' richer treasures than the mines of Mexico and of Peru '; of the Dominion's trade and government relations with the whole class of men who ' have their business in great waters '; and, finally, of that guardian Navy, without whose freely given care the ' water history ' of Canada could never have been made at all.

CHAPTER II

CANOES

WHAT the camel is to desert tribes, what the horse is to the Arab, what the ship is to the colonizing Briton, what all modern means of locomotion are to the civilized world to-day, that, and more than that, the canoe was to the Indian who lived beside the innumerable waterways of Canada. The Indian went fishing, hunting, campaigning, and sometimes even whaling, in his bark canoe. Jacques Cartier found Indians fishing in the Gulf of St Lawrence and sleeping under their upturned canoes, as many a white and Indian has slept since that long-past summer of 1534. Every succeeding explorer made use of the Indian canoe, up to the time of Mackenzie,[1] who paddled north to the Arctic in 1789, along the mighty river which bears his name ; and who, four years

---

[1] For the canoe voyages of Mackenzie, to the Arctic in 1789 and to the Pacific in 1793, see *Adventurers of the Far North* and *Pioneers of the Pacific Coast* in this Series.

later, closed the age of great discoveries by crossing the Great Divide to the westward-flowing Fraser and reaching the Pacific by way of its tributary, the Blackwater, an Indian trail overland, and the Bella Coola. Mackenzie had found the canoe route; and when he painted the following record on a fiord rock he was bringing centuries of arduous endeavour to a befitting close: 'Alexander Mackenzie, from Canada, by land, the 22nd of July, 1793.' This crowning achievement with paddle and canoe seems very far away from the reader of the twentieth century. Yet François Beaulieu, one of Mackenzie's voyageurs, only died in 1872, and was well known to many old North-Westers who are still alive.

The Indian birch-bark canoe is pre-eminently characteristic of Canada. But it is not the most primitive type of small craft; and it was often superseded for various purposes by the more advanced types introduced by the whites. There are three distinct types of small craft all the world over. Like everything else, they have followed the invariable order of evolution, from the simple to the complex. First came the simple log, which served the earliest man to cross some little stretch of water by the aid of pole or paddle. Next came

A.A.   B

the union of several logs, which formed the
clumsy but more stable raft. Then some pre-
historic genius found that the more a log was
hollowed out the better it would float; and
so the dug-out was invented. Log, raft, and
dug-out all belong to the first and simplest
type, in which there are no artificial parts to fit
together. The second type is exemplified by
the birch-bark canoe, which has three parts in
its frame—gunwale, cross-bars, and ribs—and
a fourth part, the skin, to complete it. The
third type is distinguished from the second by
its keel, as clearly as vertebrate animals are distinguished from invertebrates by their backbone. The common keeled boat, with all its
variations, represents this third and, so far,
final type. All three types have played their
parts in Canada, both jointly and separately,
and all three play their parts to-day. But they
are best understood if taken one by one.

First, then, the log, the raft, and the dug-
out canoe. Any one watching a 'log drive'
to-day can see the shantymen afloat in much the
same way, though for a very different purpose,
as their remotest human ancestors hundreds
of thousands of years ago. The raft, like the
log, is now a self-carrying cargo, not a
passenger craft. But there it is, much as it

always was. Indeed, it is simpler now than
it used to be some years ago, before the days
of tugs and railways. Then it was craft and
cargo in one. It was steered by immense oars,
as sailing vessels were before the days of
rudders; other gigantic oars were occasionally used to propel it, like an ancient galley;
it carried loose-footed square sails, like the
ships of Tarshish; and its crew lived aboard
in shacks and other simple kinds of shelter,
like the earliest Egyptian cabins ages before
the captivity of Israel.

The dug-out has the humblest, though the
longest, history of any craft the hand of man
has ever shaped. At one time it rose to the
dignity of being the liner and the man-of-war
of the Pacific coast; for the giant trees there
favoured a kind of dug-out that the savage
world has never seen elsewhere, except in
certain parts of equatorial Africa. At another
time, only a century or two ago, dug-outs of
twenty feet or so were used in trade between
the St Lawrence and the Hudson. They were
of white pine, red or white cedar, or of tulip
tree; and their crews poled standing or
paddled kneeling, for they had no thwarts.
They carried good loads, went well, with their
canoe-shaped ends, and lasted ten or twelve

years if tarred or painted. They were, indeed, one-piece canoes, which they had a perfect right to be, as the word canoe comes from the name the West Indian natives gave their dug-outs when questioned by Columbus. Nowadays the dug-out is generally used for the dirtier work of 'longshore fisheries. It has lost its elegance of form, and may be said to have reverted to a lower type. But this reversion only serves the better to remind the twentieth century of what all sorts of craft were like, not twenty, but two hundred, centuries ago.

Secondly comes the Indian bark canoe, so justly famous in the history, romance, and poetry of Canada. As in the case of other craft, its form, size, and material have never been what we call 'standardized.' Indians living outside the birch belt had to use inferior kinds of bark. But the finest type was always made, and is still made, with birch-bark. At least three kinds of tree are necessary for the best results : the birch for the skin, the fir to caulk it with, and the cedar for the sewing fibres and the frame. Only a single tool is needed—a knife ; and many a good canoe was built before the whites brought metal knives from Europe. The Indian looks out for the biggest, soundest, and smoothest birch tree in his neighbourhood. He prefers to strip it in the early summer, when the bark is supple with the sap. Sap is as good for the bark as it is bad for the woodwork of canoes and every other kind of craft. The soft inside of the bark is always scraped as clean as a tanner scrapes a hide. If the Indian has to build with dry or frozen bark he is careful to use hot water in stripping the trunk, and he warms the bark again for working. Of course, it is a great advantage to have as few strips as possible, since every seam must first be sewn together by the squaws and then gummed over. Occasionally a tree will be found big and suitable enough to yield a single strip from which a seamless twenty-footer can be built. But this is very rare.

The next thing is the frame—the gunwale, ribs, and cross-bars. Where many canoes are building there is generally some sort of model round which the ribs are bent. But a skilled Indian can dispense with any model when making the ribs with every requisite degree of curve, from the open ribs amidships, where the bottom is nearly flat, to the close ribs at the ends, where the shape becomes halfway between the letter ' U ' and the letter ' V.' The gunwale is quite the most important part of the canoe, as it holds all the other parts together and serves some of the constructional purposes of a keel. The voyageurs, recognizing this, call it *le maître*. It is laid on the ends of the ribs, which are made fast to it. Then the frame is completed by the three or more cross-bars, which keep the two sides of the gunwale from spreading apart. After this the birch-bark skin is stretched on the frame as tightly as possible, turned in over the gunwale, and clamped on there by the *faux maître* or super-gunwale. The two ends, both as sharp as an ordinary bow, are then sewn together by a sort of crisscross fibre lacing, and every hole or seam in the bark is well gummed with melted rosin. The finishing touches are equally important, each in its own way. Thin boards are laid in lengthwise, either between the ribs and the skin or over the ribs, so as to protect the bark bottom from being injured by the cargo. The ends of the canoe are reinforced inside by the Indian equivalent for a collision bulkhead. This bulkhead sometimes rises well above the gunwale and is carved like a figurehead, which accounts for its voyageur name of *le p'ti' bonhomme*. A third finishing touch, very common in earlier days, is the decoration of the outsides of both ends, which used to rise with a sharp sheer, and sometimes actually curved back. The usual decorations here were totem signs, generally made of porcupine quills, dyed in many colours, and serving the original purpose of a coat of arms.

The familiar shape has never been greatly varied, though some canoes are built on finer lines for speed, and others on fuller lines for carrying cargo. But there has always been plenty of variety in size and material. The smallest canoe would hardly hold two persons, and could be carried in one hand. The big war canoes would hold more than twenty well-armed paddlers and required four men to carry them. The very biggest canoe probably did not exceed forty feet in length, six in breadth, and two in depth amidships. Fifty men or five tons of cargo could have been carried in it. But perhaps one quite so large was never built. When white cedar and birch were not to be had, all sorts of substitutes were used. Any roots with tough fibres would do for the sewing, and any light and tough wood served its turn as a more or less efficient substitute for the white cedar framing. But elm and other alternative barks

were all bad. The elm bark was used inside
out, because the outside was too rough and
brittle for the bottom of a canoe. It made dull
paddling and never lasted the whole of a hard
season, unlike the birch-bark, which sometimes
had a life of six or seven years. The most
modern material is canvas, which is generally painted red or green. It is light, easily
repaired, and has much to recommend it,
though trappers think it gives a taint which
scares their game away. The paddles were
and are of all shapes and sizes, long and short,
broad and narrow, spoon-blade and square ;
and they were and are made of all kinds of
wood, from the lightest spruce to the much
heavier but handsomer bird's-eye maple. Sails
were and are only used with light winds dead
aft, and not often in birch-barks even then,
because there is no ' stiffness ' without a keel.

There were skin as well as bark canoes
among the Indians. But the typical skin canoe
is the Eskimo kayak. This is a shuttle-shaped
craft, about fifteen feet long and just wide
enough to let its single paddler sit flat on the
bottom. It differs from the Indian canoe in
being entirely decked over. The skin of the
grey seal, when that best of canoe skins can
be found, is carefully sewn, so as to be quite

waterproof, and then stretched as tightly as
a drumhead all over the frame, except for the
little ' well ' where the Eskimo sits with his
double-bladed paddle. As he tucks himself
in so closely that water cannot enter he does
not fear to be capsized, for he can right himself
with a sweep of his paddle. Kayaks are very
light and handy, as the frame is made either
of whalebone or spruce. The oomiak is the
Eskimo's family boat and cargo carrier, flat-
bottomed, not decked in, and sometimes big
enough for twenty people with their gear. It
is made of much the same materials.

The white man's canoes, so well known—
outside of Canada—as ' Canadian canoes,' are
partly true canoes and partly a cross between
canoes and boats. The fact that the skin
is not made of bark or hide, but of canvas,
wood, or metal, and the further innovation
that machinery is freely used, make no essential
difference, provided always that there is no
semblance of a keel. But once the keel is
introduced the whole constructional idea is
changed and the ways of savages are left
behind. A first-rate keeled canoe, built of
white cedar, brass shod and copper fastened,
fitted with air tanks and life-line, a lateen sail
and portage handles, is the very perfection

of a handy little cruiser for all sorts of inland
waters. One like this, but built of basswood,
proved quite serviceable after more than ten
years' work, in the course of which it covered
several thousand miles along the Lower St
Lawrence, where the seas are often rough and
the low-tide landings always hard.

But all similar craft, though looking like
canoes afloat, are no more like the true canoes
and kayaks in their constructional detail than
a bird is like a butterfly. The keel makes all
the difference. Everything in naval architecture springs from and is related to the keel.
'Laying the keel' means beginning the ship
in the only possible way, and 'two keels to
one' is an expression which every one under-
stands as meaning a naval preponderance in
that proportion. The keel is to the ribs of a
ship exactly what the backbone is to the ribs
of a man, and any craft built up from a keel,
no matter how small and simple it may be,
belongs to the third and apparently final type
of craft, which is as far ahead of the canoe
type as that is ahead of the dug-out, raft,
and log.

An intermediate type that once did much
service, and still does a little, is the white
man's flat-bottomed boat, which could be

paddled, rowed, or sailed, according to build
and circumstances. The common punt is the
best known form of it ; the dory by far
the handiest all round ; the cargo barge the
biggest ; and the old-fashioned ' bateau ' the
most characteristically Canadian. The modern
' bateau ' is to be found only among keeled
sailing craft. But the old ' bateau,' which
Wolfe's local transport officers spelt *battoe,*
was more of a rowboat. It was sharp at both
ends, wall-sided, and fitted with oars, poles,
and a square sail. The bottom had some sheer
—that is, it was curved up at each end—but
less than the top. Four men rowed, the fifth
steered, and three tons of miscellaneous goods
or thirty-five barrels of flour made a fair cargo.
Bateaux like this were the craft in which the
United Empire Loyalists went up the St Lawrence to settle Upper Canada. Afterwards the
size and crew were increased till the average
cargo amounted to about four tons and a
half. But the Durham boat, introduced by
American traders from the Mohawk valley,
soon became a successful rival, which was not
itself supplanted till canals enabled still larger
craft to pass from one open water to another.
The Durham was larger than the bateau ; long,
light, and shallow. It had a not quite flat

bottom and a moderate sheer in the sides. The best bateaux and Durhams were made with strong white oak bottoms and light fir sides.

The bark canoe gave place to the boat, step by step, as civilized intercourse advanced. It disappeared first from the great national highway of the St Lawrence and the Lakes, where the French began using bateaux and sailing craft as early as the seventeenth century. During the eighteenth the boat gained steadily on the canoe, which was more and more confined to the Indians. The local craft in chief civilized use on both sides during the fight for Canada was the bateau; and the best crews then and afterwards were the French-Canadian voyageurs.

But everywhere beyond the immediate spheres of French and British influence the canoe was universal. The Great West then began at the Lakes and the Mississippi, and was a land of wild adventure, rumour, and extravagant surmise. The map that formed the frontispiece to the standard authority of the time—Jefferys' *French Dominions in America* —is full of geographical romance. Once in the Kaministikwia, the map has no territorial divisions other than those between the

different tribal hunting grounds, each one of
which was watered by a hundred streams and
marked by the ' carrying places ' where the
canoes had to be ' portaged.' There lived the
' Nation of the Bear ' and the ' Nation of the
Snake,' whose special totems of course were
worked in coloured quills on every war canoe ;
and there flowed many a river ' the course of
which is uncertain.' Along the great Assini-
boine lay the ' Warrior's track from the River
of the West,' and just where the prairies ran
out into the complete unknown there was the
vista of a second Eldorado in the hopeful suggestion that ' Hereabouts are supposed to be
the Mountains of Bright Stones mentioned in
the Map of ye Indian Ochagach.'

After the Conquest the tide of trade and
settlement flowed faster and faster west ; and
with the white man's trade and settlement came
the white man's boats. At last, in 1823, Sir
George Simpson, the resident governor of the
Hudson's Bay Company, finding that canoe
transport was half as dear again as that done
with boats, ordered that boats should supersede
canoes all over the main trade routes of the
Company's vast domain. This was the death-
blow to the canoe as a real factor in Canadian
life. From that time on it has been receding

farther and farther, from waterway to waterway, at first before the white man's boat with
oars and sails, and now before his steamer.
But in distant or secluded wilds it lingers still—
the same craft to-day that it was when the Celtic
coracles were paddled on the Thames before the
Romans ever heard of England—the horse, the
ship, the moving home of those few remaining
nomads whose life is dying with its own.

The great historic age of inland small craft—
the age of dug-out, bateau, and canoe; the
age of Indian, pioneer, and voyageur—was the
eighteenth century, when fresh-water sailing
craft were few, when steamers were unknown,
and when savage and civilized men and
methods were mingled with each other in the
fur trade over a larger area than they used in
common either before that time or since. The
seventeenth century saw the slow beginnings of
this age after Champlain had founded Quebec
in 1608 and had taken the warpath with the
Hurons against the Iroquois. The nineteenth
century saw its almost equally slow decline,
which began in 1815, at the close of the war
with the United States, and may be said to
have been practically completed with the
two North-West Rebellions of 1870 and
1885. The latter year, indeed, closed a real

epoch with three significant events: the end of
the last Indian and half-breed war in Canada,
the completion of the first trans-continental
Canadian railway, and the return from Egypt
of the first and last Canadians to go on an
oversea campaign as professed voyageurs.

Under the French régime the fur trade
reached well past Lake Superior. Nepigon and
the Kaministikwia were the two most important junctions of routes at the western end
of the lake. Under British rule the Montreal
'fur lords' used the 'Grand Portage,' which
ends on a bay of Lake Superior some way south
of the modern Fort William. It was a regular
bush road, nearly ten miles long, made to avoid
the falls of the Pigeon. As early as 1783, the
year in which King George III first recognized
the United States as an independent power, the
fur lords kept no less than five hundred men
in constant work at the height of the season,
during the latter half of August. Horses and
oxen were used later on; but the voyageur
himself was the chief beast of burden here,
as everywhere else. There were two kinds
of voyageur. One was the mere merchant
carrier, who went from Montreal to the Grand
Portage in big boats of four tons burden having
a crew of ten men. These were the 'pork

eaters' or *mangeurs de lard,* who had
nothing worse to face than well-known rapids.
The others were a finer breed, the true and
daring coureurs de bois, or pioneers of the
bush, who went west in comparatively light
canoes, each carrying not more than a ton and
a half, who hunted their own game, risked a
fight with the Indians, and were to the duller
' pork eaters ' what a charger is to a cart-
horse or a frigate to a barge. The regulation
portage load was one hundred and fifty pounds,
and many a man was known to carry this
weight the whole ten miles and back within
six hours.

There was need to hurry. Supplies were
going west to Lake Winnipeg, up the Saskatchewan, and even on to Athabaska; while furs
were coming down for the autumn trade to
Europe. As a rule the traders were Scottish
and the voyageurs French Canadian. Indians
and half-breeds were fairly common; they
manned the canoes in the farther wilds,
guided the pioneers, and did the actual trap-
ping. To speak in terms of modern transportation: the Indians and their bark canoes
produced the raw material and worked the
branch lines; while the voyageurs met them
at the junctions and took the goods down to

the head of ocean navigation, where everything was, of course, trans-shipped for Europe. The same sort of trade was carried on, in a slightly different way, in the Maritime Provinces. There are survivals of it still in Labrador. At the end of July, Nascaupees, some of whom take months to reach their hunting grounds by paddle and portage, may be seen at Seven Islands, on the north shore of the Gulf of St Lawrence, where huge modern pulp mills make paper for the New York press, and where the offing is alive with transatlantic shipping all season through.

These inland voyages are as strange to the average Canadian of to-day as to contemporary Englishmen and Frenchmen. So it is perhaps worth while to record the ordinary features of what must soon become altogether a thing of the past. The incidents would be much the same with every kind of small craft that has served its turn along the interlocking network of Canadian waterways, whether an old-fashioned bateau or a Durham boat, a sharp-end dug-out, or a bark canoe. But the immemorial birch-bark is the best to choose for example, as it preceded and outlasted every other kind and is the most typically Canadian of them all.

13934

Before starting, every broken seam and hole must be gummed over. Water is poured into the canoe and every point of exit marked for gumming. Loading must be done with unusual care, as the slightest crankness of such frail craft in such wild waters is likely to prove fatal. Crews always were their own stevedores, and it was a poor crew that could not load to perfection in a short five minutes, once the cargo had been settled. The actual paddling is not difficult to learn, that is, the paddling required from an ordinary member of the crew. But the man in the bow and, still more, the man in the stern need the highest kind of skilful daring to take them safely through. Paddling by oneself also requires a special touch, only to be learnt by long practice. Even in dead water it takes some time before a novice can send the canoe straight ahead when paddling on one side only. As the paddle goes aft the bow naturally tends to turn towards the other side. The trick of it consists in counteracting this tendency by a twist of the blade which brings the inner edge round, aftwise beside the canoe, till the blade becomes a rectifying rudder as well as a thrusting propeller at the end of every stroke. When a fall or impassable rapid is reached,

the 'bowman' jumps out before the canoe
touches bottom and draws her safely ashore.
He and the 'steersman' then carry her over
the portage, while the rest carry the cargo
on their backs. A man's own weight is a fair
load; but with a sling across their foreheads,
and clasped hands behind their heads, strong
men have carried twice as much and more.
When a rapid has to be ascended the canoe is
lightened as much as need be, the steel-shod
poles are got out, and the bow and stern
paddlers stand up to their work, balancing
themselves as easily as other men would on
dry land.

But it is when a rapid is to be 'run' that the
finest skill is shown. If there is any doubt the
steersman walks down to take a good look first.
Then, if necessary, some or all of the cargo is
taken out and portaged to the next 'steady'
in the river. Rapids are so common in some
journeys that canoemen think less of them
than foxhunters think of five-barred gates.
In most cases a mistake means death; so
every nerve and muscle is kept tensely ready
the whole run through. The current should
be 'humoured'; for it does a surprising
amount of the work itself. If rightly headed
with the main throw of it the canoe will

naturally tend to seek the deepest and safest channel just as the body of the water does. Split channels must be met by instant decision; and it is when picking out the proper one that steerage way tells. As the pace of the rapid increases, so does the danger; for the slightest false thrust of a blade is enough to make a canoe swerve or upset. But, with the expert bowman on the keenest of look-outs and the course under the knowing touch of the still more expert steersman, a rapid may be run in perfect safety through racing waves which only just fail to leap aboard, on roaring water which drowns the human voice so completely that the bowman can only make use of signals, past rocks and snags on which a single graze would mean a wreck, and, often the worst of all, from one wild 'throw' to another with quite a different set and a wrench of two fierce currents where they meet.

All the white man's boats used by the voyageurs approximated more or less to the shape of the canoe: the various kinds of Hudson river dug-out, the bateau, the 'Durham,' and the 'York,' which last became the wooden successor of the birch-bark after Governor Simpson's general inspection of the Hudson's Bay domain. Only the rather barge-

like 'Mackinaw' was completely outside this
venturesome class. It was a useful but hum-
drum cargo boat, laboriously poled along
shallow, quiet waters, or rowed with lumbering sweeps; or sometimes even sailed, when
it shovelled its way through the water with a
very safe wind dead aft.

This completes the tale of Canadian inland
small craft that depended on pole and paddle,
oar and towline, and only used a simple
sail as an exceptional thing. But the human
interest would not be complete without some
reference to the tours of inspection made by
the magnates of the Hudson's Bay Company.
The greatest tours of all were those of Sir
George Simpson, the governor who took
charge after the Company absorbed its war-
ring rival in 1821. In modern business
language he would be called the executive
head of the great Canadian fur-trade 'merger.'
He was a young promoted clerk, a Scotsman
born, with little experience of the Canadian
wilds, but with the natural faculty of rule and
a good deal of diplomacy—the gauntlet in the
velvet glove.

Simpson soon grasped the salient features of
the people he had to deal with and very sensibly
made his tours of inspection as much like a

royal progress as he could. Time and money
were never neglected: his ' record runs '
across the wilderness and the dividends at
headquarters proved that to the full. He
was determined to show every one concerned
that thenceforth there was only one governing
company, and that he was its proper representa-
tive. Then, as always, London was the general
headquarters. But the Canadian headquarters
were at Montreal; and Simpson fixed what might
be called the field headquarters at Norway
House, near the north end of Lake Winnipeg,
a commanding strategic point in the heart of
the great fur territories. Here he was always
busy introducing discipline, enforcing a much-
needed reduction in the ration of rum given
to the Indians, and reporting home. As
voyageurs, he thought the French Canadians
much better than the men of any other race.
' Canadians preferable to Orkneymen. Orkneymen less expensive but slow. Less physical
strength and spirits. Obstinate if brought
young into the service. Scotch and Irish,
when numerous, quarrelsome, independent,
and mutinous.' He introduced fines as a
punishment. But ' this will only do for
Europeans. A blow is better for Canadians.'

On July 12, 1828, Simpson left York Factory

on Hudson Bay for a state and business
progress across the continent to Fort Vancouver on the Columbia. One of his staff,
Archibald Macdonald, wrote an account of it,
called *Peace River: a Canoe Voyage from
the Hudson Bay to the Pacific*. The best of
birch-barks were used to ensure speed; though
the birch-bark had already been superseded
as a cargo craft. There was a doctor in the
party, which included nine voyageurs to each
of the two canoes. Simpson's departure was
the signal for a salute of seven guns, which
was duly repeated at every subsequent fort.
The whole population lined the waterside as
the voyageurs struck up one of their old French
folk-songs to beguile the way. The arrival
at Norway House was still more imposing.
The Union Jack, with the magic letters ' H. B. C.'
on its fly, was hoisted, to the admiration of all
the whites and Indians from that most important neighbourhood. Simpson's party had
landed out of sight to put on their best clothes;
after which they shot through the gorge at
full speed, to the strains of the bagpipes from
Simpson's canoe and bugles from the other.
At Fort St James, the central point of ' New
Caledonia,' the approach was made by land.
' Unfurling the British Ensign, it was given

to the guide, who marched first. After him came the band, consisting of buglers and bagpipers. Next came the governor, mounted, and behind him Hamlyn and Macdonald, also on horses. Twenty men loaded like beasts of burden formed the line, and finally M'Gillivray with his wife and family brought up the rear.' On the nineteenth day out from York Factory Simpson reached Fort Langley at the mouth of the Fraser.

How far away it all seems now in this new twentieth century! And yet, as in the case of Alexander Mackenzie, there is a wonderfully intimate human link connecting that time with our own; for Lord Strathcona was born before the amalgamation of the rival compan es in 1821; he became the last resident-governor of the Hudson's Bay Company while François Beaulieu, Mackenzie's centenarian voyageur, was still alive; and he lived until 1914, the year of the Great World War.

CHAPTER III

SAILING CRAFT: THE PIONEERS

WHEN we call Canada a new country in the twentieth century we are apt to forget that her seafaring annals may possibly go back to the Vikings of the tenth century, a thousand years ago. Long before William the Conqueror crossed over from France to England the Vikings had been scouring the seas, north, south, east, and west. They reached Constantinople; they colonized Iceland; they discovered Greenland; and there are grounds for suspecting that the ' White Eskimos' whom the Canadian Arctic expedition of 1913 noted down for report are some of their descendants. However this may be, there is at least a probability that the Vikings discovered North America five centuries before Columbus. The saga of Eric the Red sings of the deeds of Leif Ericson, who led the discoverers and named the three new countries Helluland, Markland, and Vineland. Opinions differ as to which

of the four—Labrador, Newfoundland, Nova
Scotia, or New England—are to be included
in the Vikings' three. In any case, the only
inevitable two are Newfoundland and Nova
Scotia, with which the subsequent history of
Canada also begins.

But even if the Vikings never came to Canada
at all, their ships could not be refused a place
in any history of sailing craft ; for it is the
unique distinction of these famous freelances
of the sea to have developed the only type of
ancient and mediaeval hull which is the admiration of the naval world to-day. The kind of
vessel they used in the tenth century is the
craft of most peculiar interest to Canadian
history, though it has never been noticed
there except by the merest landsman's reference. The special type to which this vessel
belonged was already the result of long
development. The Vikings had a way of
burying a chief in his ship, over which they
heaped a funeral mound. Very fortunately
two of these vessels were buried in blue clay,
which is an excellent preserver of timber ; so
we are able to see them to-day in an almost
perfect state. The one found in 1880 at the
mouth of the Christiania fjord is apparently
a typical specimen, though smaller than many

that are described in the sagas. She is about eighty feet long, sixteen feet in the beam, and seven feet in total depth amidships, from the top of the gunwale to the bottom of the keel. The keel runs into the stem and stern-post with very gentle curves. The whole of the naval architecture is admirably done. The lines are so fine that there is almost the least possible resistance to the water when passing through it. The only point worth criticizing is the slightness of the connection between the topsides and the body of the boat. But as this was a warship, carrying little besides live ballast, such a defect would be minimized. Iron rivets, oak treenails (or pegs), clinker planking (each plank-edge overlapping the next below it), admirably proportioned frame, as well as arrangements for stepping, raising, and lowering the single mast, all show that the builders knew exactly what they were about.

The rudder is hung over on the starboard, or ' steer-board,' side and worked by a tiller. The ropes are made of bark fibre and the planking is partly fastened to the floors with ties made of tough tree roots. Only one sail, and that a simple square one, was used. Nothing could be done with this unless the wind was more or less aft. The sail, in fact, was centuries behind the hull, which, with the firm grip of its keel, would have been quite fit for a beat to windward, if the proper canvas had been carried. The thirty oars were often used, and to very good purpose, as the easy run of the lines suited either method of propulsion. The general look of these Viking craft is not unlike that of a big keeled war canoe, for both ends rise with a sharp sheer and run to a point. A classical scholar would be irresistibly reminded of the Homeric vessels, not as they were in reality, but as they appear in the eager, sea-born suggestions of the Iliad and the Odyssey — long, sharp, swift, well-timbered, hollow, with many thwarts, and ends curved high like horns.

Three Viking vessels discovered in a Danish peat-bog probably belong to the fifth century, thus being fifteen hundred years of age. Yet their counterparts can still be seen along the Norwegian coast. Such wonderful persistence, even of such an excellently serviceable type, is quite unparalleled; and it proves, if proof were needed, that the Norsemen who are said to have discovered Newfoundland and Nova Scotia were the finest seamen of their own and many a later time. The way they planned and built

SHIPS OF THE FIFTEENTH CENTURY

From Winsor's *America*

their vessels was the glory of their homes. The way they manned and armed and fought them was the terror of every foreign shore. War craft and crew together were the very soul and body of strength and speed and daring skill, as, with defiant figurehead and glittering, shield-hung sides, they rode to battle joyously on the wild white horses of the mediaeval sea.

Five centuries more, and the English, another great seafaring people, first arrived in Canada. Then came increasing swarms of the most adventurous fishermen of Europe. After these came many competing explorers and colonizers, all of whose fortunes directly depended on the sea.

Cabot's English crew of eighteen hands is a century nearer to our own time than Leif Ericson the Norseman was to Cabot's. Yet Cabot himself preceded Columbus in setting foot on what may fairly be called the mainland of America when he discovered Canada's eastern coast in 1497. He cleared from Bristol in May, reached the new regions on June 24, and returned safe home at the end of July. It was an age of awakening surmise. The universal question was, which is the way to the golden

East ? America was looked upon as a rather annoying obstruction to proper navigation, though it was allowed to have some incidental interest of its own. Vasco da Gama doubled the Cape of Good Hope in the same year that Cabot raised St George's Cross over what afterwards became British territory. Twenty-five years later Magellan found the back way through behind Cape Horn, and his ship, though not himself, went round the world. Then, twelve years later still, the French sailed into the Canadian scene on which they were to play the principal part for the next two centuries and a quarter.

Every text-book tells us that Jacques Cartier was the great French pioneer and explains his general significance in the history of Canada. But no books explain his peculiar significance from the nautical point of view, though he came on the eve of the most remarkable change for the better that was ever made in the art of handling vessels under sail. He was both the first and the last mediaeval seaman to appear on Canadian inland waters. Only four years after his discovery of the St Lawrence, an Englishman, Fletcher of Rye, astonished the seafaring world of 1539 by inventing a rig with which a ship could beat to windward with sails trimmed fore and aft. This invention introduced the era of modern seamanship. But Cartier has another, and much more personal, title to nautical fame, for he was the first and one of the best of Canadian hydrographers, and he wrote a book containing some descriptions worthy of comparison with those in the official ' Pilots ' of to-day. This book, well called his *Brief Recit et Succincte Narration*, is quite as easy for an Englishman to read in French as Shakespeare is for a Frenchman to read in English. It abounds in acute observations of all kinds, but particularly so in its sailing directions. Compare, for instance, his remarks on Cumberland Harbour with those made in the latest edition of the *St Lawrence Pilot* after the surveys of four hundred years. Or take his few, exact, and graphic words about Isle-aux-Coudres and compare them with the entries made by the sailing masters of the British fleet that used this island as a naval base during the great campaign for the winning of Canada in 1759. In neither case will Cartier suffer by comparison. He was captain, discoverer, pilot, and surveyor, all in one; and he never failed to make his mark, whichever rôle he undertook.

Like all the explorers, Jacques Cartier had his

troubles with his crews. The average man
of any time cannot be expected to have the
sustained enthusiasm, much less the mani-
fold interest, which inspires his leader. Nearly
every commander of the fifteenth, sixteenth,
and seventeenth centuries had to face mutiny ;
and, even apart from what might be called
natural causes, men of that time were quite
ready to mutiny for what seem now the most
absurd of reasons. Some crews would not
sail past the point of Africa for fear of turning
black. Others were distracted when the wind
held for days together while they were outward
bound, lest it might never blow the other way
in North America, and so they would not be
able to get back home. The ships, too, often
gave as much trouble as the men. They were
far better supplied with sails and accommodation than the earlier Viking ships had been ;
but their hulls were markedly inferior. The
Vikings, as we have seen, anticipated by centuries
some of the finest models of the modern world.
The hulls of Cabot, Columbus, and Cartier were
broader in the beam, much bluffer in the bow,
besides being full of top-hamper on the deck.
Nothing is known about Cabot's vessel except
that she must have been very small, probably
less than fifty tons, because the crew numbered

only eighteen and there was no complaint of being short-handed. Cartier's *Grande Hermine* was more than twice as large, and, if the accepted illustrations and descriptions of her may be relied upon, she probably was not unlike a smaller and simplified *Santa Maria*, the ship which bore Columbus on his West Indian voyage of 1492. Such complete and authentic specifications of the *Santa Maria* still remain that a satisfactory reproduction of her was made for the Chicago World's Fair of 1893. Her tonnage was over two hundred. Her length of keel was only sixty feet; length of ship proper, ninety-three; and length over all, one hundred and twenty-eight. This difference between length of keel and length over all was not caused by anything like the modern overhang of the hull itself, which the Vikings had anticipated by hundreds and the Egyptians by thousands of years, but by the box-like forecastle built over the bows and the enormous half and quarter decks jutting out aft. These top-hampering structures over-burdened both ends and produced a regular see-saw, as the Spanish crew of 1893 found to their cost when pitching horribly through a buffeting head sea. The *Santa Maria*, like most 'Spaniards,' had a lateen-rigged mizzen.

But the *Grande Hermine* had no mizzen, only the square-rigged mainmast, foremast, and bowsprit. The bowsprit of those days was a mast set at an angle of forty-five; and it sometimes, as in the *Grande Hermine*, carried a little upright branch mast of its own.

Many important changes occurred in the nautical world during the two generations between the days of Jacques Cartier and those of Champlain. The momentous change in trimming sails, already referred to, came first, when Fletcher succeeded in doing what no one had ever done before. There can be no doubt that the lateen sail, which goes back at least to the early Egyptians, had the germ of a fore-and-after in it. But the germ was never evolved into a strong type fit for tacking; and no one before Fletcher ever seems to have thought it possible to lay a course at all unless the wind was somewhere abaft the beam. So England can fairly claim this one epoch-making nautical invention, which might be taken as the most convenient dividing-line between the sailing craft of ancient and of modern times.

The French had little to do with Canada for the rest of the sixteenth century. Jacques Cartier's best successor as a hydrographer was

Roberval's pilot, Saint-Onge, whose log of
the voyage up the St Lawrence in 1542 is full
of information. He more than half believes
in what the Indians tell him about unicorns
and other strange beasts in the far interior.
And he thinks it likely that there is unbroken
land as far as Tartary. But, making due
allowance for his means of observation, the
claim with which he ends his log holds good
regarding pilotage : ' All things said above
are true.'

The English then, as afterwards, were always
encroaching on the French wherever a seaway
gave them an opening. In 1578 they were
reported to be lording it off Newfoundland,
though they had only fifty vessels there, as
against thirty Basque, fifty Portuguese, a
hundred Spanish, and a hundred and fifty
French. Their numbers and influence increased year by year, till, in 1600, they had two
hundred sail manned by eight thousand men.
They were still more preponderant farther north
and farther south. Frobisher, Davis, Hudson,
and other Englishmen left their mark on what
are now Arctic and sub-Arctic Canada. Hudson
also sailed up the river that bears his name,
and thus did his share towards founding the
English colonies that soon began their ceaseless

struggle with New France. But even before his time, which was just after Champlain had founded Quebec, two great maritime events had encouraged the English to aim at that command of the sea which they finally maintained against all rivals. In 1579 Sir Francis Drake sailed completely round the world. He was the first sea captain who had ever done so, for Magellan had died in mid-career fifty-seven years before. This notable feat was accompanied by his successful capture of many Spanish treasure ships. Explorer, warrior, enricher of the realm, he at once became a national hero. Queen Elizabeth, a patriot ruler who always loved a hero for his service to the state, knighted Drake on board his flagship; and a poet sang his praises in these few, fit words, which well deserve quotation wherever the sea-borne English tongue is known:

> The Stars of Heaven would thee proclaim,
>   If men here silent were.
> The Sun himself could not forget
>   His fellow traveller.

Nine years later the English Navy fought the unwieldy Spanish Armada into bewildered flight and chased it to its death round the hostile coast-line of the British Isles.

Meanwhile the quickened interest in 'sea affairs' had led to many improvements in building, rigging, and handling vessels. Surprising as it may seem, most of these improvements were made by foreigners. Still more surprising is the fact that British nautical improvements of all kinds, naval as well as mercantile, generally came from abroad during the whole time that the British command of the sea was being won or held. Belated imitation of the more scientific foreigner was by no means new, even in the Elizabethan age. It had become a national habit by the time the next two centuries were over. English men, not English vessels, won the wars. The Portuguese and Spaniards had larger and better vessels than the English at the beginning of the struggle, just as the French had till after Trafalgar, and the Americans throughout the War of 1812. Even Sir Walter Raleigh was belated in speaking of the 'new' practice of striking topmasts, 'a wonderful ease to great ships, both at sea and in the harbour.'

CHAPTER IV

SAILING CRAFT: UNDER THE FLEURS-DE-LIS[1]

EVERY one knows that when Champlain stood beside Lake Huron, wondering if it had a western outlet towards Cathay, he was discovering the Great Lakes, those fresh-water seas whose area far exceeds the area of Great Britain. Every one knows that he became the 'Father of New France' when he founded Quebec in 1608; and that he was practically the whole civil and military government of Canada in its infant days. But few know that he was also a captain in the Royal Navy of France, an expert hydrographer, and the first man to advocate a Panama canal. And fewer still remember that he lived in an age which, like our own, had

[1] The nautical history of New France is all parts and no whole; brilliant ideas and thwarted execution; government stimulus and government repression; deeds of daring by adventurers afloat and deeds of various kinds by officials ashore: everything unstable and changeable; nothing continuous and strong. It cannot, therefore, make a coherent narrative, only a collection of half-told tales.

CHAMPLAIN'S SHIP, THE *DON DE DIEU*

From the model at the Quebec Tercentenary

its 'record-breaking' events at sea. Baffin's
'Farthest North,' reached in 1616, was latitude
77° 45'. This remained an unbroken record
for two hundred and thirty-six years. Champlain's own voyage from Honfleur to Tadoussac in eighteen days broke all previous records,
remained itself unbroken for a century, and
would be a credit to a sailing ship to-day.
His vessel was the *Don de Dieu*, of which he left
no exact description, but which was easily
reproduced for the tercentenary of Quebec in
1908 from the corresponding French merchant
vessels of her day. She was about a hundred
tons and could be handled by a crew of twenty.
The nearest modern equivalent of her rig is
that of a barque, though she carried a little
square sail under her bowsprit and had no
jibs, while her spanker had a most lateenish
look. Her mainsail had a good hoist and
spread. She had three masts and six sails altogether. The masts were 'pole,' that is, all of
one piece. The tallest was seventy-three feet
from step to truck, that is, from where the
mast is stepped in over the keel to the disc that
caps its top. She carried stone ballast; her
rudder was worked by a tiller, with the help
of a simple rope tackle to take the strain; and
the poop contained three cabins.

Not long after the death of Champlain (1635)
there was a world-wide advance in shipbuilding. Perhaps it would not be too much to say
that the modern school of wooden sailing-ship
designers began with Phineas Pett, who was
one of a family that served England well for
nearly two hundred years. He designed the
Sovereign of the Seas, which brought English
workmanship well to the front in the reign of
Charles I. She surpassed all records, with a
total depth from keel to lanthorn of seventy-
six feet, which exceeds the centre line, from
keel to captain's bridge, of modern ' fliers '
with nearly twenty times her tonnage. The
Cromwellian period also gave birth to a most
effective fleet, which in its turn was succeeded
by the British fleets that won the Second
Hundred Years' War with France and decided
the destiny of Canada. This long war, or series
of wars, begun against Louis XIV in the seventeenth century, only ended with the fall of
Napoleon at Waterloo. La Hogue in 1692,
Quebec in 1759, and Trafalgar in 1805 were three
of the great deciding crises. La Hogue and
Trafalgar were purely naval; while Quebec
was the result of a joint expedition in which
the naval forces far exceeded the military. The
general effect of this whole Second Hundred

Years' War was to confirm the British command of the sea for another century.

But the French designs in shipbuilding were generally better than the English. The French, then and afterwards, were more scientific, the English more rule-of-thumb. Yet when it came to actual handling under sail, especially in action, the positions were reversed. The English seafaring class was far larger in proportion to population and it had far more practice at sea. Besides, England had more and more at stake as her oversea trade and empire extended, till at last she had no choice, as an imperial power, but either to win or die.

The French kingdom rose to its zenith under Louis XIV, whose great minister, Colbert, did all he could to foster the Navy, the mercantile marine, and the French colonies in Canada. But the fates were against him. France was essentially a landsman's country. It had several land frontiers to attack or defend, and it used its Navy merely as an adjunct to its Army. Moreover, its people were not naturally so much inclined to colonize oversea possessions as the British, and its despotic colonial system repressed all free development. The result was that the French dominions in America never reached a population of one hundred thousand. This was insignificant compared with the twelve hundred thousand in the British colonies ; while the disparity was greatly increased by the superior British aptness for the sea.

French Canada had all the natural advantages which were afterwards turned to such good account by the British. It had timber and population along a magnificently navigable river system that tapped every available trade route of the land. Had there only been a demand for ships New France might have also enjoyed the advantage of employing the scientific French naval architects. But the seafaring habit did not exist among the people as a whole. A typical illustration is to be found in the different views the French and British colonists took of whaling. The British on Nantucket Island first learned from the Indians, next hired a teacher, in the person of Ichabod Paddock, a famous whaling master from Cape Cod, and then themselves went after whale with wonderful success. The French in Canada, like the British on Nantucket Island, had both whales and whaling experts at their very doors. The Basques kept a station at Tadoussac, and whales were seen at Quebec. But, instead of hiring Basques to teach them, the French in Canada petitioned the king for a subsidy with which to hire the Basques to do the whaling for them. Of course the difference between the two forms of government counts for a good deal—and it is not at all likely that any paternal French ruler, on either side of the Atlantic, ever wished to encourage a sea-roving spirit in Canada. But the difference in natural and acquired aptitude counts for more.

The first Canadian shipbuilding was the result of dire necessity. Pont-Gravé put together a couple of very small vessels in 1606 at Port Royal so that he might cruise about till he met some French craft homeward bound. Shipbuilding as an industry arose long after this. The *Galiote*, a brigantine of sorts, was built by the Sovereign Council and launched at Quebec in 1663. But it was the intendant Talon who began the work in proper fashion. In 1665, immediately after his arrival, he sent men ' timber-cruising ' in every likely direction. Their reports were most encouraging. Suitable timber was plentiful along the waterways, and the cost was no more than that of cutting and rafting it down to the dockyards. Talon reported home to Colbert. But official correspondence was too slow. At his own cost he at once built a vessel of a hundred and twenty tons. She was on the most approved lines, and thus served as a model for others. A French Canadian built an imitation of her the following year. Talon vainly tried to persuade this enterprising man to form a company and build a ship of four hundred tons for the trade with the West Indies. Three smaller vessels, however, successfully made the round trip from Quebec to the West Indies, on to France, and back again, in 1670. In 1671 Colbert laid aside for Talon a relatively large sum for official shipbuilding and for the export of Canadian wood to France. The next year Talon had a five-hundred-tonner on the stocks, while preparations were being made for an eight-hundred-tonner, which would have been a ' mammoth ' merchant vessel in contemporary France. Before he left Canada he had the satisfaction of reporting that three hundred and fifty hands, out of a total population of only seven thousand souls, were engaged in the shipyards.[1] But there were very few at sea.

The first vessel to sail the Great Lakes was built by La Salle seventy years after their discovery by Champlain. This was *Le Griffon*,

[1] See in this Series *The Great Intendant*, chapters iv and ix.

which, from Father Hennepin's description, seems to have been a kind of brig. She was of fifty or sixty tons and apparently carried a real jib. She was launched at the mouth of Cayuga Creek in the Niagara peninsula in 1679. Her career was interesting, but short and disastrous. She sailed west across Lake Erie, on through Lakes St Clair and Huron, and reached Green Bay on Lake Michigan, where she took in a cargo of fur. On her return voyage she was lost with all hands.

In the eighteenth century shipbuilding in Quebec continued to flourish. The yards at the mouth of the St Charles had been enlarged, and even then there was so much naval construction in hand that private merchant vessels could not be built as fast as they were wanted. In 1743 some French merchants proposed building five or six vessels for the West India trade, besides twenty-five or thirty more for local trade among the West Indian islands. A new shipyard and a dry-dock were hurriedly built; and there was keen competition for ship-carpenters. In 1753 *L'Algonkin*, a frigate of seventy-two guns, was successfully launched. The shipwrights experimented freely with Canadian woods, of which the white oak proved the best. But the Canadian-built vessels for

transatlantic trade never seem to have equalled
in number those that came from France.

The restrictions on colonial trade were rigidly
enforced; no manufacture of goods was allowed
in the colonies, and no direct trade except
with France and French possessions. Canada
imported manufactured goods and exported
furs, timber, fish, and grain. The deep-water
tonnage required for Canada was not over ten
or twelve thousand, distributed among perhaps
forty vessels on the European route and twenty
more that only visited the French West Indies.
A complete round trip usually meant a cargo of
manufactures from France to Canada, a cargo
of timber, fish, and grain from Canada to the
West Indies, and a third cargo—of sugar,
molasses, and rum—from the West Indies
home to France. Quite half the vessels, however, returned direct to France with a Canadian
cargo. Louisbourg was a universal port of call,
the centre of a partly contraband coasting trade
with the British Americans, and a considerable
importing point for food-stuffs from Quebec.

French commerce on the sea had, however,
a mighty rival. The encroaching British were
working their way into every open water in
America. The French gallantly disputed their
advance in Hudson Bay and won several

actions, of which the best victory was Iberville's in 1697, with his single ship, the *Pélican*, against three opponents. In Labrador and Newfoundland the British ousted all rivals from territorial waters, except from the French Shore. The 'Bluenose' Nova Scotians crept on from port to port. The Yankees were as supreme at home as the other British were in Hudson Bay, though on occasion both were daringly challenged. All the French had was the line of the St Lawrence; and that was increasingly threatened, both at its mouth and along the Great Lakes.

The British had in their service a powerful trading corporation. The Hudson's Bay Company was flourishing even in the seventeenth century. In one sense it was purely maritime, as its posts were all on the Bay shore, while the French traded chiefly in the hinterlands. The Company's fleet, usually three or four ships, sailed regularly from Gravesend or Portsmouth about June 1, rounded the Orkneys and made for Hudson Bay. The return cargo of furs arrived home in October. This annual voyage continues to the present day.[1]

---

[1] For the narrative of the Hudson's Bay Company the reader is referred to *The Adventurers of England on Hudson Bay,* in this Series.

As Hudson Bay was the place for fur, so Newfoundland, and all the waters round it, was the place for fish. 'Dogs, fogs, bogs, and codfish,' was the old half-jeering description of its products. Standing in the gateway of Canada, Newfoundland was always a menace to New France. Thirty years before Champlain founded Quebec a traveller notes that, among the fishing fleets off Newfoundland, 'the English rule all there.' In other quarters, too, there was a menace to France. The British colonies were always feeling their way along the coast as well as along the Great Lakes. In spite of ordinances on both sides, forbidding trade between colonies of different powers, little trading craft, mostly British, would creep in with some enticing contraband, generally by way of Lake Champlain.

The first attempt in the English colonies to trade with Canada by way of the open sea was made in 1658, when Captain John Perel sailed from New York for Quebec in the French barque *St Jean*, and was wrecked on Anticosti, with the total loss of a cargo of sugar and tobacco. The sloop *Mary* managed to reach Quebec in 1701 with a miscellaneous cargo, containing, among many other items, '166 cheses, 20+81+101 Rols of tobacko,

A FRENCH FRIGATE OF THE EIGHTEENTH CENTURY

From Winsor's *America*

2 hogheds of botls marckt SR, 70 bunches of arthen waire pots, 8 barels of beaire, 19 caskes of schotte.' Her return cargo included ' 14 barels of brandy, 4 hogsds of Claret, 2 bondles of syle skins, etc.' She was wrecked before she reached home, but most of her cargo was saved. Her owner, Samuel Vetch, the son of a ' Godly Minister and Glorifier of God in the Grass Market ' in Edinburgh, was a great local character in New York. Four years after this voyage he was sent to Quebec to arrange a truce between New France and New England. But his return was as unlucky as that of his sloop *Mary*, for he was arrested and fined £200 on a charge of having traded with his own country's official enemies.

The fashion in ships changed very slowly. As we have seen, what may be called the ancient period of sailing ships closed about the time Jacques Cartier appeared in Canada. When the fore-and-aft-trimmed sails were invented in 1539, the modern age began. This has three distinctive eras of its own. The first lasted for about a century after the time of Jacques Cartier; and its chief work was to free itself of ancient and mediaeval limitations. The second, or central, modern era lasted twice

as long, from the middle of the seventeenth
century to the middle of the nineteenth. It
thus covered one century under the Fleurs-de-
lis in Canada and another under the Union
Jack. It also exactly corresponded with the
long era of the famous British navigation laws,
of which more will presently be heard. During
this period sails were improved in size, cut, and
setting. The changes can be described only
in technical language. Jibs became universal,
adding greatly to handiness in general and the
power of tacking in particular. Four sails were
used on a mast—main, top, topgallant, and
royal. Naval architecture was greatly improved,
especially by the French. But this improvement
did not extend to giving the hull anything like its
most suitable shape. The Vikings were still
unbeaten in this respect. Even the best foreign
three-deckers were rather lumbering craft.

The third era began with the introduction
of the clippers about 1840, and will not
end till deep-sea sailing craft cease to be
a factor in the world's work altogether.
It was in this present era, when steamers
were gaining their now unquestioned victory,
and not during previous eras, when steam
was completely unknown, that sailing craft
reached their highest development. Sails in-

creased to eight on the mainmast of a full-rigged ship, and they were better cut and set than ever before. Yachts and merchantmen cannot be fairly compared in the matter of their sails. But it is worth noting that the old 'white-winged days' never had any sort of canvas worth comparing with a British yacht-ing 'Lapthorn' or a Yankee yachting 'Sawyer' of our own time. Hulls, too, have improved far beyond those of the old three-decker age, beyond even the best of the Vikings'.

Such broad divisions into eras of shipbuilding are, of course, only to be taken as marking world-wide nautical advances in the largest possible sense. One epoch often overlaps another and begins or ends at different times in different countries. A strangely interesting survival of an earlier age is still to be seen along the Labrador, in the little Welsh and Devonshire brigs, brigantines, and topsail schooners which freight fish east away to Europe. These vessels make an annual round: in March to Spain for salt; by June along the Labrador; in September to the Mediterranean with their fish; and in December home again for Christmas. They are excellently handled wherever they go; and no wonder, as every man aboard of them is a sailor born and bred.

CHAPTER V

SAILING CRAFT: UNDER THE UNION JACK

WHEN Canada finally became a British possession in 1763 she was, of course, subject to the navigation laws, or the Navigation Act, as this conglomeration of enactments was usually called. The avowed object of these laws was to gain and keep the British command of the sea. They aimed at this by trying to have British trade done in British ships, British ships manned by British crews, and British crews always available if wanted for British men-of-war. The first law was enacted under the Commonwealth in 1651. The whole series was repealed under Victoria in 1849. Exceptions were often made, especially in time of war; and there was some opposition to reckon with at all times. But, generally speaking, and quite apart from the question of whether they were wise or not, the British government invariably looked upon these navigation laws as a cardinal point of policy down to the close of the wars with the French Empire and the American Republic in 1815.

The first laws only put into words what every sea-power had long been practising or trying to practise : namely, the confining of all sea trading to its own ships and subjects. They were first aimed at the Dutch, who fought for their carrying trade but were crushed. They operated, however, against all foreigners. They forbade all coastwise trade in the British Isles except in British vessels, all trade from abroad except in British ships or in ships belonging to the country whence the imported merchandise came, all trade between English colonies by outsiders, and all trade between the colonies and foreign countries, except in the case of a few enumerated articles. The manning clauses were of the same kind. Most of the crew and all the officers were to be British subjects—an important point when British seamen were liable to be ‘pressed’ into men-of-war in time of national danger.

The change of rule in 1763 meant that Canada left an empire that could not enforce its navigation laws and joined an empire that could. Whatever the value of the laws, Canadian shipping and sea trade continued to grow under them. In the eighteenth century

there was little internal development anywhere
in America; and less in Canada than in what
soon became the United States. People worked
beside the waterways and looked seaward for
their profits. Elias Derby, the first American
millionaire, who died in 1799, made all his
money, honestly and legally, out of shipping.
Others made fortunes out of smuggling. An
enterprising smuggler at Bradore, just inside
the Strait of Belle Isle, paved his oaken stairs
with silver dollars to keep the wood from
wearing out; and he could well afford to
do so.

The maritime provinces of Nova Scotia
(then including New Brunswick) and Prince
Edward Island had been gradually growing
for a quarter of a century before the United
Empire Loyalists began to come. Halifax
was a garrison town and naval station. There
was plenty of fish along the coast; and the
many conveniently wooded harbours naturally
invited lumbering and shipbuilding. Fish and
furs were the chief exports up to the War of
1812; after that, timber. The Loyalists came
in small numbers before 1783; in larger
numbers during the five years following.
From twenty to thirty thousand altogether are
said to have settled in the Maritime Provinces.

They were poor, but capable and energetic, and by the end of the eighteenth century their 'Bluenose' craft began to acquire a recognized place at sea. Quebec and Montreal did an increasing business. Quebec was the great timber-trade and shipbuilding centre; Montreal the point where furs were collected for export. From Quebec 151 vessels took clearance in 1774. In 1800 there were 21 Quebec-built vessels on the local register. Ten years later there were 54.

The Great Lakes had no such early development. Moreover, the days of their small beginnings were full of retarding difficulties. Nor were they free from what was then a disaster of the first magnitude; for in 1780 a staggering loss happened to the infant colony. The *Ontario* foundered with one hundred and seventy-two souls on the lake after which she was named. During the fourteen years between the Conquest and the Revolution only a few small vessels appeared there. On the outbreak of the Revolution the British government impressed crews and vessels alike, and absolutely forbade the building of any craft bigger than an open boat except for the government service. Subsequently the strained relations on both sides, lasting till after the War of

1812, and the tendency of the Americans to encroach on the frontier trade and settlements, combined to prevent the government from giving up the power it had thus acquired over shipping. The result was that trade was carried on in naval vessels, some of which had originally been built as merchantmen and others as men-of-war. There were frequent complaints of non-delivery from the business community, both on the spot and in England. But ' defence was more important than opulence,' and the burden was, on the whole, cheerfully borne by the Loyalists. In 1793 twenty-six vessels cleared from Kingston. Two years later a record trip was made by the sloop *Sophia*, which sailed from there to Queenston, well over two hundred miles, in eighteen hours. Two years later again a traveller counted sixty wagons carrying goods from Queenston, beyond the other end of Lake Ontario, to Chippawa, so as to get them past Niagara Falls. Anywhere west from Montreal the unit of measurement for all freight was a barrel of rum, the transport charge for which was over three dollars as far as Kingston, where it was trans-shipped from the bateau to a schooner.

There was very little shipping on Lake Erie

till after the War of 1812. The first American
vessel launched in these waters had a curious
history. After a season's work in 1797 she
was carted past Niagara and launched on Lake
Ontario, where she plied between Queenston
and Kingston under the British flag with the
name of *Lady Washington*. The rival Hudson's
Bay and North-West Companies each had a
few boats on the western Lakes at the beginning of the nineteenth century, and the government maintained there a tiny flotilla of its own.
But shipping was a very small affair west of
Niagara for several years to come.

While the War of 1812 killed out the feeble
trade on the Lakes, it greatly stimulated the
well-established trade in sea-going craft from
Quebec and the Maritime Provinces. The
British command of the sea had become so
absolute by 1814 that the whole American coast
was practically sealed to trade, which was thus
forced to seek an ' underground ' outlet by
way of Canada, in spite of the state of war.
This, in addition to the transport required by
the British forces in Canada, sent freights and
tonnage up by leaps and bounds. The only
trouble was to find enough ships and, harder
still, enough men.

Canadian sailing craft in the nineteenth

century had a chequered career. Many disturbing factors affected the course of trade: the cholera of '32; the Rebellion of '37; the Ship Fever of '47; the great gold finds in California in '49 and in Australia in '53; Reciprocity with the United States in '54; Confederation in '67; the triumph of steam and steel in the seventies; and the era of inland development which began in the eighties.

The heyday of the Canadian sailing ship was the third quarter of the nineteenth century. This period, indeed, was one of great activity in the history of mast and sail all the world over. There was intense rivalry between steam and sail. The repeal of the Navigation Act in England had brought the whole of British shipping into direct competition with foreigners. The Americans were pushing their masterful way into every sea. The rush to California was drawing eager fleets of Yankee, Bluenose, and St Lawrence vessels round the Horn. India, China, and Australia were drawing other fleets round the Cape. The American clippers threatened to oust the slower 'Britishers' and throw the comparatively minor Canadians into the shade. For the first and only time in history American tonnage actually began to threaten British supremacy.

But the challenge was met in the proper way, by building to beat on even terms. The British had already regained their lead before the Civil War of the sixties; and the subsequent inland development of the United States, with the momentous change from wood and sails to steel and steam, combined to depress the American mercantile marine in favour of its British rival.

Canada played a great part in this brief but stirring era, when the wooden sailing vessel was making its last gallant stand against steam, and the sun of its immemorial day was going down in a blaze of glory which will never fade from the memories of those who love the sea. Canada built ships, sailed ships, owned ships, and sold ships. She became one of the four greatest shipping centres in the world; and this at a time when she had less than half as many people and less than one-tenth as much realized wealth as she has now. Quebec had more than half its population dependent on ship-building in the fifties and sixties. In 1864 it launched sixty vessels, many of them between one and two thousand tons. About the same time Nova Scotia launched nearly three hundred vessels and New Brunswick half as many. The Nova Scotians, however, only averaged two hundred tons, and the New Brunswickers four hundred. If the Lakes, Prince Edward Island, the rest of Canada, and Newfoundland are added in, the total tonnage built in the best single year is found to be close on a quarter of a million. Allowing for the difference in numbers of the respective populations, this total compares most favourably with the highest recent totals built in the British Isles, where the greatest shipbuilding the world has ever seen is now being carried on.

It was the change from wood to metal that caused the decline of shipbuilding in Canada. It was also partly the change to steam ; but only partly, for Canada started well in the race for building steamships. What proves that the disuse of wood was the real cause of the decline is the fact that Canada never even attempted to compete with other countries in building metal sailing vessels. If Canada had developed her metal industries a generation sooner she would have had steel clippers running against 'Yankees,' 'Britishers,' and German ' Dutchmen ' ; for there was a steel-built sailing-ship age that lasted into the twentieth century and that is not really over yet. Indeed, even wooden and composite sailers are still at work ; and with their steel comrades they still make a very large fleet. Singular proof of this is sometimes found. Nothing collects sailing ships like a calm; vessels run into it from all quarters and naturally remain together till the breeze springs up. But, even so, most readers will probably be surprised to learn that, only a few years ago, a great calm off the Azores collected a fleet of nearly three hundred sail.

Canadian shipbuilders had some drawbacks to contend with. One was of their own making. Certain builders in the Maritime Provinces, especially at Pictou and in Prince Edward Island, turned out such hastily and ill constructed craft as to give 'Bluenoses' a bad name in the market. By 1850, however, the worst offenders were put out of business, and there was an increasing tendency for the builders to sail their own vessels instead of selling them.

A second, and this time a general, drawback was the difficulty of getting Canadian-built vessels rated A1 at Lloyd's. 'Lloyd's,' as every one knows, is the central controlling body for most of the marine insurance of the world, and its headquarters are in London. There were very few foreign 'Lloyd's' then, and no colonial; so it was a serious matter when the

English Lloyd's looked askance at anything not built of oak. Canada tried her own oak; but it was outclassed by the more slowly growing and sounder English oak. Canada then fell back on tamarac, or 'hackmatac,' as builders called it. This was much more buoyant than oak, and consequently freighted to advantage. But it was a soft wood, and Lloyd's was slow to rate it at its proper worth. Tamarac hulls went sound for twenty years, and sometimes forty, especially when hardwood treenails were used—a treenail being a bolt that did the service of a nail in woodwork or a rivet in steel plating. At first Canadian vessels were only rated A1 for seven years, as compared with twelve for those built of English oak. A year was added for hardwood treenails, and another for 'salting on the stocks.' In 1852 Lloyd's sent out its own surveyor, Menzies, who would guarantee work done under his own eye for twenty-five cents a ton; while Lloyd's, for its part, would give preferential rates to any vessels thus 'built under special survey.' Perhaps Canadian timber is not as lasting as the best European. Certainly it has no such records of longevity; though there is no reason why Canadian records should not be better than they are in this respect. Few people know how long a well-built and well-cared-for ship can live. Lloyd's register for 1913 contains vessels launched before Queen Victoria began to reign. Merchantmen have often outlived their century. Nelson's *Victory* still flies the flag at Portsmouth, though she was laid down the year before Wolfe took Quebec. And the *Konstanz*, a thirty-five-ton sloop, still plies along the Danish coast, although her launch took place in 1723—a hundred and ninety years ago.

A third drawback for Canadian builders was the lack of capital. Shipbuilding fluctuates more than most kinds of business, and requires great initial outlay as well; so failures were naturally frequent. The firm of Ross at Quebec did much to steady the business by sound finance. But the smaller yards were always in difficulties, and no shipbuilder ever made a fortune.

Excellent craft, however, came out of Canadian yards : notable craft wherever they sailed. One of the best builders at Quebec was a French Canadian, whose beautiful clipper ship *Brunelle*, named after himself, logged over fourteen knots an hour and left many a smart sailer, and steamer too, hull down astern. Mackenzie of Pictou was builder and skipper both. With the help of a friend he began by cutting down the trees and doing all the rest of the work of building a forty-five-ton schooner. By 1850 he had built a fourteen-hundred-tonner, the famous *Hamilton Campbell Kidston*, which greatly astonished Glasgow, for she was then the biggest ship the Clyde had ever seen. His last ship was launched in the ' record ' year of 1865. The Salter Brothers did some fine work at the ' Bend,' as Moncton was then called. Their first vessel, a barque of eight hundred tons, was sold at once in England. Next year they built a clipper ship called the *Jemsetgee Cursetgee* for an East Indian potentate, who sent out an Oriental figurehead supposed to be a likeness of himself. A peculiar feat of theirs was rigging as a schooner and sending across the Atlantic a scow-like coal barge ordered by a firm in England.

The decline of Canadian sailing craft was swifter than its rise ; and with the sailing craft went the Canadian-built steamers, because wood was the material used for both, and the use of iron and steel in the yards of the British Isles soon drove the wooden hulls from the greater highways of the sea. Once the palmy days of the third quarter of the century were over the decline went on at an ever-increasing rate. In 1875 Canada built nearly 500 vessels, and, if small craft are included, the tonnage must have nearly reached 200,000. In 1900 she built 29 vessels, of 7751 tons—steam, steel, wood, and sail. Shipowning does not show such a dramatic contrast, but the decline has been very marked. Within twenty-two years, from 1878 to 1900, the Canadian registered tonnage was almost exactly halved. The drop was from a grand total, sail and steam together, of a million and a third, which then made Canada the fourth shipowning country in the world and put her ahead of many nations with more than ten times her population.

CHAPTER VI

SAILING CRAFT: THE BUILDING OF THE SHIP

SHIPBUILDING was and is a very complex industry. But only the actual construction can be noticed here, and that only in the briefest general way. The elaborate methods of European naval yards were not in vogue anywhere in Canada, not even in Quebec, much less in Nova Scotia. It was not uncommon for a Bluenose crew to make everything themselves, especially in the smaller kinds of vessels. They would cut the trees, draft the plan, build the ship and sail her: being thus lumbermen, architects, builders, and seamen all in one. The first step in building is to lay the blocks on which the keel itself is laid. These blocks are short, thick timbers, arranged in graduated piles, so that they form an inclined plane of over one in twenty, from which the completed hull can slide slowly into the water, stern first. Then comes the laying of the keel, that part which is to the whole vessel what the backbone is to a man. A false keel is added to the bottom of this in order to increase its depth and consequent grip. This prevents the side drift which is called making leeway. The false keel is only fastened to the keel itself from underneath, because such a fastening is strong enough to resist water pressure and weak enough to allow of detachment in case of grounding. The slight projection of the keel itself then gives too little purchase for a dangerous amount of leverage on the frame. A long keel is made up of several pieces of square timber, with their ends shaped into scarfs, an overlapping and interlocking arrangement of great strength. The foremost keel piece is scarfed into the stem, which is the fore-end of the vessel's bow. The aftermost keel piece joins the stern-post, on which the rudder hangs. Elm makes a good keel, especially with oak for stem and stern-post.

The frame, to pursue our simile, is to the ship what ribs are to our bodies. In the same way the planking is the skin. The frame, or ribs, determines the vessel's form. There were, and still are, many varieties of frame. In a very small vessel there are very few timbers. The keel is probably all in one piece, and the planks may possibly run from stem

to stern without a break. In this case the
unity of each piece supplies enough longitudinal
resistance to strains. But when a vessel is
large, and more especially when she is long,
the strains known as hogging and sagging are
apt to rack her timbers apart.

A ship is not built for mere passive resistance, like a house, or even for resistance
only to pressures and vibrations, like a bridge.
She is built to resist every imaginable strain of
pitching and rolling, and so requires archi-
tectural skill of a far higher kind than is required (in the constructional, not the aesthetic,
sense) for any structure on the land. When a
ship is on the top of a single wave she tends to
hog, because there is much less support for
her ends than for her centre, and so her ends
dip down, racking her upper and compressing
her lower parts amidships. When the seas
are shorter she often has her ends much
more waterborne than her centre, and this
in spite of the fact that the extreme ends are
not naturally waterborne themselves. Then
she sags, and the strains of racking and compressing are reversed, because her centre tends
to sink and her ends to rise. Now, a series of
hogging and sagging strains alternately com-
presses and opens every resisting join in every

timber, with the inevitable result of loosening
the whole. To meet these strains longitudinal
strength must be supplied. The keel supplies
much of it, so does the planking (or skin) to a
lesser degree; but not enough; and the ribs, by
themselves, are for transverse stiffening only.
Four means are therefore employed to hold
the parts together lengthwise—keelsons, shelf-
pieces, fillings, and some form of truss.

The keelson is an inverted keel inside the
vessel. The floors, which are the timbers
uniting the two sides of the frame (or ribs),
are given a middle seating on the keel. The
keelson is then placed over them, exactly in
line with the keel, when bolts as long as the
thickness of all three are used to unite the
whole in one solid backbone, and this backbone with the ribs. Side or 'sister' keelsons
were used in the Navy on either side of the
mainmast for a distance equal to about a third
of the length of the keelson. But they were
little used in merchant vessels, and their
longitudinal resistance was only partial and
incidental. Shelf-pieces and waterways were
adapted from French models by Sir Robert
Seppings, who became chief constructor to
the Navy some years after Trafalgar. They are
thick timbers running continuously under and

over the junctions of the deck beams with the ship's sides, to both of which they are securely fastened.

The keelson was an old invention and shelf-pieces and waterways were soon in vogue. But fillings and trusses, both expensive improvements, were not much favoured in any mercantile marine. The truss is even older than the keelson, having been used by the ancient Egyptians at least thirty-five centuries ago, and probably earlier. Four to eight pillars rose in crutches from the bottom amidships to about six feet above the gunwale. The Egyptians ran a rope over the crutches and round the mast, and then used its ends to brace up the stem and stern. The moderns discarded the rope, took the strains on connecting timbers, and modified the truss, sometimes out of recognition. But many Canadian and American river steamers of the twentieth century A.D. employ the same principle for the same object as the Egyptians of the seventeenth century B.C. Fillings came from the French, like shelf-pieces and waterways. Seppings put them between the ribs, in the form of thick timbers. The whole frame thus became almost solid against any tendency of the ribs to close together, and quite strong enough against their other tendency to draw apart.

All means that strengthen a well-built hull longitudinally have also been made to add their quota to its transverse strength. The ribs spring from the solid mass of their own floors bolted in between the keelson and the keel; and the planking, or skin, is let into the rabbets, or side grooves, of the keel and firmly fastened to the ribs throughout by hardwood pegs called treenails. The decks are, in themselves, a source of weakness. The beams supporting them are like the rafters of a house, which, of course, work the walls apart under pressure from the floors—and here, as in every other detail, the stability required for a house is nothing to what is required for a ship. The way to overcome this difficulty is to make the decks and beams so many bridges holding the sides together. At the point of junction of every beam-end with a shelf-piece, waterway, and rib there is an arrangement of bolts and dowellings (or dovetailings) which makes the whole as solid as possible. An extra bolt through the waterway, rib, and outside planking adds to the strength; and a knee, or angular piece of wood or iron connecting the shelf with the under side of the beam, almost completes the

beam-end connection. The final touches are
the clamps below the shelves and the spirketing
above the waterways, with short-stuff between
the clamps of one deck and the spirketing of
the next below.

All this is only the merest suggestion of
what is done for the main part of the vessel's
hull. The ends require many modifications,
because the shape there approaches a V, and
so the floors cannot cross the keel as holding
bodies. But the breast-hooks forward and
crutches aft, the deck transom, which is the
foundation for the deck abaft as well as the
assemblage of timbers uniting the stern to
the body of the vessel, with all the other parts
that make up the ends, cannot be more than
mentioned here. Then come the decks, which
are quite complex in themselves, and still more
complex by reason of the mast-holes and
hatchways cut out of them all, and the windlass, bitts, and capstan built into the one that
is exposed to the storm. To make sure that
whatever strength is taken out by cutting is
restored in some other way, and that the
exposed deck which has to resist the strains
put upon the structures built into it is specially
reinforced, the most careful provision must be
made for the mast-holes; for the hatchways

with their coamings fore and aft on carlings
that reach from beam to beam; for the riding
bitts, which are posts to hold the cable when
the vessel is at anchor, and which must
therefore be immensely strong; for the windlass, which in the merchant service often did
the double duty of the bitts and capstan; and
for a multiplicity of other parts.

A landsman could hardly believe what a
marvellous adjustment of co-operating parts
is required for a ship unless he actually watches
its construction. He will then understand
why it is by far the most wonderful structure
man has ever built throughout all the ages of
his evolution.   It represents his first success in
mastering an element not his own; and, whatever the future may see in the way of aviation,
the priority of seamanship will always remain
secure by thousands and thousands of known
and unknown years.

But we are still no farther than a few parts
of the hull.   There is the stepping of the masts,
with their heels set firm and square above the
keel, and their rake ' right plim ' throughout.
Then there is the whole of the rigging—a
perfect maze to look at, though an equally
perfect device to use ; the sails, which require
the most highly expert workmanship to make ;

the rudder, and many other essentials. Finally, there is all that is needed in every well-found vessel which is 'fit to go foreign.' No vessel would go far unless its under-water parts were either sheathed, tarred, or tallowed; for sea-worms burrow alarmingly, and 'whiskers' grow like the obnoxious weeds they are. These particulars, of course, leave many important gaps in the process.

Then the hull has to be transferred from the inclined plane of block piles, on which it was built, to a cradle, on which it moves down the sliding-ways into the water.

When everything is ready, the christening of the ship takes place. A bottle of wine is broken against her bows and her name is pronounced by some distinguished person in a formula which varies more or less, but which is generally some version of the good old English benediction: 'God bless the *Dreadnought* and all who sail in her.' No matter what the name may be, the ship herself is always 'she.' Many ingenious and mistaken explanations have been given of this supposedly female 'she.' The schoolboy 'howler' on the subject is well known: 'All ships are "she" except mail boats and men-of-war.' Had this schoolboy known a very little more he might have added jackass brigs to his list of male exceptions. The real explanation may possibly be that the English still spoken at sea is, in some ways, centuries older than the English spoken on land, and that the nautical ' she ' comes down to us from the ancient days in which all inanimate objects were endowed with life in everyday speech and neuters were as yet unknown.

Immediately this most stirring ceremony ceases, the stentorian order comes to ' Down dog-shore ! ' on which the dog-shore trigger is touched off, the dog-shores fall, an awakening quiver runs through the sliding-ways and cradle ; and then the whole shapely vessel, still facing the land from which she gets her being, moves majestically into the water, where her adventurous life begins.

CHAPTER VII

SAILING CRAFT: 'FIT TO GO FOREIGN'

WE will suppose that the ship is complete in hull, successfully launched, and properly rigged and masted. The two questions still remaining are: what is her crew like, and how does she sail?

The typical British North American crew of the nineteenth-century sailing ship is the Bluenose crew. Newfoundlanders were too busy fishing in home waters, though some of them did ship to go foreign and others sailed their catch to market. Quebeckers built ships, but rarely sailed them; while the Pacific coast had no shipping to speak of. Thus the Bluenoses had the field pretty well to themselves. Bluenoses were so called because the fog along the Nova Scotian and New Brunswick coast was supposed to make men's noses bluer than it did elsewhere. The name was generally extended by outsiders to all sorts of British North Americans; and, of course, was also applied

SHIP *BATAVIA*, 2000 TONS

Built by F.-X. Marquis at Quebec, 1877. Lost on Inaccessible Island, 1879

From a picture belonging to Messrs Ross and Co., Quebec

to any vessel, as well as any crew, that hailed from any port in British North America, because a vessel is commonly called by the name of the people that sail her. 'There's a Bluenose,' 'that's a Yankee,' 'look at that Dago,' or 'hail that Dutchman' apply to ships afloat as well as to men ashore. And here it might be explained that 'Britisher' includes anything from the British Isles, 'Yankee' anything flying the Stars and Stripes, 'Frenchie' anything hailing from France, 'Dago' anything from Italy, Spain, or Portugal, and 'Dutchman' anything manned by Hollanders, Germans, Norsemen, or Finns, though Norwegians often get their own name too. A 'chequer-board' crew is one that is half white, half black, and works in colour watches.

Hard things have often been said of Bluenose crews. Like other general sayings, some of them are true and some of them false. But, mostly, each of them is partly true and partly false : and—'circumstances alter cases.' The fact is, that life aboard a Bluenose was just what we might expect from crews that lived a comparatively free-and-easy life ashore in a sparsely settled colony, and a very strenuous life afloat in ships which depended, like all ships, on disciplined effort for both success and safety. When national discipline is not very strong ashore it has to be enforced by hook or by crook afloat. The general public never bothered its head much about seamen's rights or wrongs in a rather ' hard ' new country managing its own maritime affairs. So there certainly were occasional ' hell ships ' among the Bluenoses, though very rarely except when there were Bluenose officers with a foreign crew.

This was quite in accordance with the practice all along the coast of North America. Even aboard the famous Black Ball Line of Yankee transatlantic packets in the forties there was plenty of ' handspike hash ' and ' belaying-pin soup ' for shirkers or mutineers. The men before the mast were mostly foreigners and riff-raff Britishers ; very few were Yankees or Bluenoses. Discipline had to be maintained ; and it was maintained by force. But these were not the real hell ships. ' Hell ships ' were commonest among deepwatermen on long voyages round the Horn, or among the whalers when the best class of foremast hands were not to be had. Many of them are much more recent than is generally known ; and even now they are not quite extinct. ' Black Taylor,' ' Devil Summers,' and ' Hell-fire

Slocum' are well within living memory.
Black Taylor came to a befitting end. Because the rope surged at the capstan he kicked
the nearest man down, and was jumping to
stamp his ribs in, when the man suddenly
whipped out his knife and ripped Black Taylor
up with a New Orleans nigger trick-twist for
which he got six months, though really deserv-
ing none.

But such mates and skippers always were
exceptions ; and, as a general rule, no better
crews and vessels have ever sailed the sea
than the Yankees at their prime. Their
splendid clippers successfully challenged the
slower Britishers on every trade route in the
world. At the very time that the *America* was
beating British yachts hull-down, the old
British East Indiamen were still wallowing
along with eighty hands to a thousand tons,
while a Yankee thousand-tonner could sail
them out of sight with forty. The British
excuse was that East Indiamen required a
fighting crew as well as a trading one, and that
British vessels were built to last, not simply
put together to make one flashy record. But
after the Napoleonic wars the British Navy
could police the world of waters ; so double
numbers were no longer needed ; and if East

Indiamen were built to last, how was it they
only went an average of six times out and six
times home before being broken up ?

Nor was it only in speed that the Yankees
were so far ahead. They paid better wages,
they gave immeasurably better food, they were
smarter to look at and smarter to go, their
rigging was tauter, their sails better cut and
ever so much flatter on a wind, their cargo
more quickly and scientifically stowed, and,
most important point of all, their discipline
quite excellent. Woe betide the cook or steward
whose galley or saloon had a speck of dirt
that would make a smudge on the skipper's
cleanest cambric handkerchief ! It was the
same all through, from stem to stern and keel
to truck, from foremast hand to skipper.
Aboard the best clippers the system was well-
nigh perfect. Each man had found, or had the
chance of finding, the position for which he
was most fit. The best human combination
of head and heart and hand was sure to come
to the top. The others would also find their
own appropriate levels. But shirkers, growlers,
flinchers, and mutineers were given short
shrift. The officers were game to the death
and never hesitated to use handspikes, fists, or
firearms whenever the occasion required it.

As for sea-lawyers—the canting equivalent of ranting demagogues ashore—they could hardly have got a hearing among any first-rate crew. No admiralissimo ever was a greater hero to a junior midshipman than the best Yankee skippers were to the men before the mast. There's no equalitarian nonsense out at sea.

This digression springs from and returns to the main argument; because the Yankee excellence is so little understood and sometimes so grudgingly acknowledged by British and foreign landsmen, and because Bluenose and Yankee circumstances and practice were so much alike. Britishers were different in nearly all their natural circumstances, while, to increase the difference, their practice became greatly modified by a deal of good but sometimes rather lubberly legislation. And yet all three—Britisher, Bluenose, and Yankee—are so inextricably connected with each other that it is quite impossible to understand any one of them without some reference to the other two.

Bluenose discipline was good, very good indeed. When the whole ship's company was Bluenose discipline was partly instinctive and mostly went well, as it generally did when Yankees and Bluenoses sailed together. The whole population of the little home port—

men, women, and children — knew every
vessel's crew and all about them. The men
were farmers, fishermen, lumbermen, shipbuilders, and 'deepwatermen,' often all in one.
Among other peoples, only Scandinavians ever
had such an all-round lot as this. Even in
the present century, with its increasing multi-
formity of occupation, books full of nauticalities
can be read and understood in these countries
by everybody, though such books cannot be read
elsewhere except by the seafaring few. Business meant ships or shipping ; so did politics,
peace and war, adventure and ambition.

But there is a different tale to tell when the
tonnage outran the Bluenose ability to man
it, and Dutchmen, Dagos, miscellaneous wharf-
rats, and 'low-down' Britishers had to be
taken on instead. If the crew was mixed and
the officers Bluenose there was sure to be
trouble of graduated kinds, all the way up
from simple knock-downs to the fiercest gun-
play of a real hell ship. The food was inferior
to that aboard the Yankees. But in discipline
there was nothing to choose. An all-Bluenose
or all-Yankee sometimes came as near the
perfection of seamanship and discipline as
anything human possibly can. But aboard
a mixed Bluenose the rule of bend or break

was enforced without the slightest reference
to what was regarded as landlubber's law.
The Britisher's Board of Trade regulations
were regarded with contempt ; and not without reason ; for, excellent as they were, they
struck the Bluenose seamen as being an inter-
ference made solely in the supposed interests
of the men against the officers.

The mistake was that the old injustices were
repeated in a new way. Formerly the law
either sided with the officers and owners
or left them alone ; now it either sided with
the men or left the officers and owners in the
lurch. The true balance was not restored.
Here is a thoroughly typical instance of the
difference between a Britisher and a Bluenose
under the new dispensation. The second mate
of a Britisher asked for his discharge at Bombay
because he could not manage the men, who
had shirked disgracefully the whole way out.
The skipper got a good Bluenose for his new
second mate. The first day the Bluenose
came aboard one of the worst shirkers slung
a bucket carelessly, cut the deck, and then
proceeded to curse the ship and all who sailed
in her, as he had been accustomed to do under
the Britisher. The Bluenose mate simply
said, ' See here, just shut your head or I 'll

shut it for you,' on which the skulker answered
by threatening to ' cut his chicken liver out.'
In a flash the Bluenose had him naped, slung,
and flying across the rail. A second man
rushed in, only to be landed neatly on the chin
and knocked limp against the scuppers. The
rest of the watch, roused by this unwonted
assertion of authority, came on, but stopped
short, snarling, when the Bluenose swung an
iron bar from the windlass in a way that
showed he knew how to handle it effectively.
The skipper and mate now appeared, and,
seeing a clear case of actual fight, at once
ranged themselves beside the capable Bluenose.
The watch, a mixed lot, then slunk off; and,
from that day out, the whole tone of the ship
was changed, very much for the better.

It is pleasanter, however, to take our last
look at a Bluenose vessel, under sail, with
Bluenose skipper, mates, and crew, and a
Bluenose cargo, all complete. But a word
must first be said about other parts and other
craft, lest the Maritime-Province Bluenose
might be thought the only kind of any consequence. There were, and still are, swarms
of small craft in Canada and Newfoundland
which belong mostly or entirely to the fisheries,
and which, therefore, will be noticed in another

chapter. The schooners along the different coasts, up the lower St Lawrence, and round the Lakes; the modern French-Canadian sailing bateaux; the transatlantic English brigs that still come out to Labrador; the many Britishers and Yankees that used to come to Bluenose harbours and to Quebec; the foreigners that come there still; and the host of various miscellaneous little vessels everywhere—all these are by no means forgotten. But only one main thread of the whole historic yarn can be followed here.

Before starting we might perhaps remember what a sailing vessel cannot do, as well as what she can, when the proper men are there and circumstances suit her. She is helpless in a calm. She needs a tow in crowded modern harbours or canals. She can only work against the wind in a laborious zigzag, and a very bad gale generally puts her considerably off her course. But, on the other hand, she could beat all her best records under perfect modern conditions of canvas, scientific metal hull, and crew; and the historic records she actually has made are quite as surprising as they are little known. Few people realize that ' ocean records ' are a very old affair, even in Canada, where they begin with Champlain's voyage of

eighteen days from Honfleur to Tadoussac and
end with King George V's sixty-seven hours
from land to land, when he speeded home in
H.M.S. *Indomitable* from Champlain's tercentenary at Quebec in 1908, handling his
shovel in the stokehole by the way.

Here are some purely sailing records worth
remembering. A Newfoundland schooner, the
Grace Carter, has sailed across to Portugal, sold
her fish there, gone to Cadiz for all the salt that
she could carry, and then reported back in Newfoundland within the month. A Canadian
schooner yacht, the *Lasca*, has crossed easterly,
the harder way, in twelve days from the St
Lawrence. In 1860 the Yankee *Dreadnought*
made the Atlantic record by going from Sandy
Hook to Liverpool in nine days and seventeen
hours, most of the time on the rim of a hurri-
cane. Six years later the most wonderful sea
race in history was run when five famous
clippers started, almost together, from the
Pagoda Anchorage at Fu-chau for the East
India Docks in London. This race was an all-
British one, as the civil war, the progress of
steam everywhere except in the China trade,
and the stimulus of competition, had now given
Britishers the lead in the East, while putting
them on an even footing with Yankees in the

West. The course was sixteen thousand miles ; the prize was the world's championship in clipper - racing. Three ships dropped considerably astern. But the *Ariel* and *Taeping* raced up the Channel side by side, took in their pilots at the same time, and arrived within eight minutes of each other. The *Ariel* arrived first ; but the *Taeping* won, as she had left twenty minutes later. The total time was ninety-nine days. A very different, but still more striking, record is the longest daily run ever made entirely under sail. This was, in one sense at least, an Anglo-American record ; for the ship, appropriately called the *Lightning*, was built by that master craftsman, Donald M'Kay of Boston, and sailed by a British crew. She made no less than 436 sea miles, or 502 statute miles, within the twenty-four hours.

There are no individual Bluenose rivals of these mighty champions. But the Bluenoses more than held their own, all round, in any company and on any sea. So it is well worth our while to end this story of a thousand years—from the Vikings till to-day—by going aboard a Bluenose vessel with a Bluenose crew when both were at their prime.

The *Victoria* is manned by the husbands, fathers, sons, and brothers of the place where she was built. Her owners are the leaders of the little neighbourhood, and her cargo is home-grown. She carries no special carpenter and sailmaker, like a Britisher, because a Bluenose has an all-round crew, every man of which is smart enough, either with the tools or with the fid and palm and needle, for ordinary work, while some are sure to be equal to any special job. She of course carries two suits of canvas, her new best and older second best. Each sail has required more skill than tailors need to make a perfect fit in clothes, because there is a constant strain on sails, exceeding, if possible, the strains on every other part. But before sail is made her anchor is hove short, that is, the ship is drawn along by her cable till her bows are over it. 'Heave and she comes!' 'Heave and she must!' 'Heave and bust her!' are grunted from the men straining at the longbars of the capstan, which winds the tightening cable in. 'Click, click, clickety, click' go the pawls, which drop every few inches into cavities that, keeping them from slipping back, prevent the capstan from turning the wrong way when the men pause to take breath. 'Break out the mud-hook!' and a tremendous combined effort ensues. Presently a sudden welcome slack shows that the flukes have broken clear. The anchor is then hove up, catted, and fished.

'All hands make sail!' sings out the mate. The wind is nicely on the starboard quarter, that is, abaft the beam and forward of the stern, which gives the best chance to every sail. A wind dead aft, blanketing more than half the canvas, is called a lubber's wind. A soldier's wind is one which comes square on the beam, and so makes equally plain sailing out and back again. What sail a full-rigged ship can carry! The Yankee *Great Republic* could spread nearly one whole acre of canvas to the breeze. Another Yankee, the *R. C. Rickmers*, the largest sailing vessel in the world to-day, exceeds this. But her tonnage is much greater, more than eleven thousand gross, and her rig is entirely different. A full-rigged clipper ship might have twenty-two square sails, though it was rare to see so many. In addition she would have studding-sails to wing her square sails farther out. Then, there were the triangular jibs forward and the triangular staysails between the masts, with the quadrangular spanker like an aerial rudder on the lower mizzenmast. All the nine staysails would have the loose lower corner made fast to a handy place on deck by a sheet (or rope) and the fore and aft points connected by the stays to the masts, the fore point low and the aft high. This is not the nautical way of saying it. But 'points' and 'corners' and other homely land terms sometimes save many explanations which, in their turn, lead on to other explanations.

The heads of square sails are made fast to yards, which are at right angles to the masts on which they pivot. Sails and yards are raised, lowered, swung at the proper angle to catch the wind, and held in place by halliards, lifts, braces, and sheets, which can be worked from the deck. Sheets are ropes running from the lower corners of sails. All upper sails have their sheets running through sheave-holes in the yardarms next below, then through quarter-blocks underneath these yards and beside the masts, and then down to the deck. Braces are the ropes which swing the yards to the proper angle. Halliards are those which hoist or lower both the yards and sails. The square sails themselves are controlled by drawlines called clew-garnets running up from the lower corners, leechlines running in diagonally from the middle of the outside edges, buntlines running up from the foot, and spilling lines, to spill the wind in heavy

weather. When the area of a sail has to be
reduced, it is reefed by gathering up the head,
if a square sail, or the foot, if triangular, and
tying the gathered-up part securely by reef
points, that is, by crossing and knotting the
short lines on either side of this part. The
square sails on the mainmast are called, when
eight are carried, the mainsail, lower and upper
maintopsails, lower and upper maintopgallants,
main-royal, main-skysail, and the moonsail.
The standing rigging is the whole assemblage
of ropes by which the masts are supported.

These few words are very far from being a
technically full, or even quite precise, description. But, taken with what was pre-
viously said about the hull, they will give a
better general idea than if the reader was asked
to make a realizable whole out of a mazy
bewilderment embracing every single one of
all the multitudinous parts.

'All hands make sail!' Up go some to
loose the sails aloft, while others stay on deck
to haul the ropes that hoist the sails to the
utmost limit of the canvas. The jibs and
spanker generally go up at once, because they
are useful as an aid to steering. The staysails
generally wait. The jibs and staysails are
triangular, the spanker a quadrangular fore-

and-after. The square sails made fast to wide-spreading yards are the ones that take most hauling. But setting the sails by no means ends the work at them. Trimming is quite as important. Every time there is the slightest shift in the course or wind there ought to be a corresponding shift of trim so as to catch every breath the sail can hold. To effect this with the triangular sails a sheet must be slacked away or hauled more in ; while, in the case of the square sails on the yards, a brace must be attended to.

Our Bluenose mate now thinks he can get more work from his canvas. His voice rings out : ' Weather crossjack brace ! ' which means hauling the lowest and aftermost square sail more to windward. ' Weather crossjack brace ! ' sings out the timekeeper, whose duty it is to rouse the watch as well as strike the bells that mark the hours and halves. The watch tramp off and lay on to the weather brace, the A.B.'s (or able-bodied seamen) leading and the O.S.'s (ordinary seamen) at the tail. Some one slacks off the lee braces and sings out ' Haul away ! ' Then the watch proceed to haul, with weird, wild cries in minor keys that rise and fall and rise again, like the long-drawn soughing of the wind itself. *Eh—*

heigh—o—ai! Eh—heigh—ee! Eh—hugh!
In comes the brace till the trim suits the mate,
when he calls out ' Turn the crossjack brace ! '
which means making it fast on a belaying pin.
The other braces follow. By the time the topgallant braces are reached only two hands are
needed, as the higher yards are naturally much
lighter than the lower ones.

Sheets and braces are very dangerous things
to handle in a gale of wind. Every movement
of the rope must be closely watched with one
vigilant eye, while the other must be looking
out for washing seas. The slightest inattention to the belaying of a mainsheet while men
are hanging on may mean that it breaks loose
just as the men expect it to be fast, when away
it goes, with awful suddenness and force,
dragging them clean overboard before their
instinctive grip can be let go. The slightest
inattention to the seas may mean an equally
fatal result. Not once, nor twice, but several
times, a whole watch has been washed away
from the fore-braces by some gigantic wave,
and every single man in it been drowned.

Squalls need smart handling. Black squalls
are nothing, even when the ship lays over till
the lee rail's under a sluicing rush of broken
water. But a really wicked white squall

requires luffing, that is, bringing her head so
close to the wind that it will strike her at the
acutest angle possible without losing its pressure in the right direction altogether.   The
officer of the watch keeps one eye to windward,
makes up his mind what sail he 'll shorten,
and then yells an order that pierces the wind
like a shot, ' Stand by your royal halliards ! '
As the squall swoops down and the ship heels
over to it he yells again, ' Let go your royal
halliards, clew 'em up and make 'em fast ! '
Down come the yards, with hoarse roaring
from the thrashing canvas.   But then, if no
second squall is coming, the mate will cut the
clewing short with a stentorian ' Masthead the
yards again ! ' on which the watch lay on
to the halliards and haul—*Ahay ! Aheigh !
Aho—oh !* Up she goes !

The labour is lightened, as hand labour
always has been lightened, by singing to the
rhythm of the work.   The seaman's working
songs are chanties, a kind of homespun poetry
which, once heard to its rolling music and the
sound of wind and wave, will always bring
back the very savour of the sea wherever it is
heard again.   There are thousands of chanties
in scores of languages, which, like the men who
sing them, have met and mingled all round the

world.   They are the folklore of a class apart,
which differs, as landsmen differ, in ways and
speech and racial ambition, but which is also
drawn together, as landsmen never have been,
by that strange blend of strife and communing
with man and nature which is only known at
sea.   They will not bear quotation in cold print,
where they are as pitiably out of place as an
albatross on deck.   No mere reader can feel
the stir of that grand old chanty

> Hurrah ! my boys, we're homeward bound !

unless he has heard it when all hands make
sail on leaving port, and the deck begins
pulsating with the first throb of the swell that
sets in landward across the bar.   And what
can this chorus really mean to any one who has
never heard it roared by strong male voices
to the running accompaniment of seething
water overside ?

> What ho, Piper ! watch her how she goes !
> Give her sheet and let her rip.
> We're the boys to pull her through.
> You ought to see her rolling home ;
> For she's the gal to go
> In the passage home in ninety days
> From Cal-i-for-ni-o !

But though you can no more wrest a chanty
from its surroundings and then pass it off as a

seaman's folk-song than you can take the blue
from the water or the crimson from the sunset,
yet, as some chanties have become so well
known ashore, as others so richly deserve to
be known there, and as all are now being
threatened with extinction, perhaps a few
may be mentioned in passing. *Away for Rio!*
with its wild, queer wail in the middle of its
full-toned chorus, has always been a great
favourite afloat:

> For we 're bound for Rio Grande,
> And away Rio ! ay Rio !
> Sing fare-ye-well, my bonny young girl,
> We 're bound for Rio Grande.

The *Wide Missouri* is a magnificent song
for baritones and basses on the water:

> Oh, Shenando'h, I love your daughter,
>   'Way-ho, the rolling river !
> Oh, Shenando'h, I long to hear you,
>   'Way-ho, we 're bound away,
>   Down the broad Missouri.

A famous capstan chanty is well known on
land, whence, indeed, it originally came:

> And it 's hame, dearie, hame ; oh ! it 's hame I want to be.
> My topsails are hoisted and I must out to sea ;
> But the oak and the ash and the bonnie birchen tree,
> They 're all a-growin' green in the North Countree.

—which is quite as appropriate to the *Nova*

Scotia as to the one beyond the North Atlantic.
A favourite sail-setting chanty is

> *Solo.* Haul on the bowlin', the fore and maintop bowlin'—
> *Chorus.* Haul on the bowlin', the bowlin' haul!

A good pumping-out chanty after a storm is

> *Solo.* Old Storm has heard the angel call.
> *Chorus.* To my ay! Old Storm along!

Reuben Ranzo is a grand one for a good
long haul. The chorus comes after every line,
striking like a squall, with a regular roar on
the first word, Ranzo.

> *Solo.* Hurrah for Reuben Ranzo!
> *Chorus.* Ranzo, boys, Ranzo!

Ranzo's progress from a lubberly tailor to a
good smart sailor is then related with infinite
variations, but always with the same gusto.
Ranzo is only really popular afloat. But
Blow the man down is a universal favourite.

> *Solo.* Blow the man down, blow the man down,
> *Chorus.* 'Way-ho! Blow the man down.
> *Solo.* Blow the man down from Liverpool town;
> *Chorus.* Give us some wind to blow the man down.

When every sail is set and every stitch
is drawing, there is no finer sight the sea
can show. The towering masts; the canvas
gleaming white, with its lines of curving

A.A.   H

beauty drawn by the touch of the wind ; the
whole ship bounding forward as if just slipped
from her leash—all this makes a scene to stir
the beholder then and for ever after. The
breeze pipes up. She 's doing ten knots now ;
eleven, twelve ; and later on, fifteen. This
puts the lee rail under ; for she lays over on
her side so far that her deck is at a slope
of forty-five. Her forefoot cuts through the
water like the slash of a scimitar ; while her
bows throw out two seething waves, the windward one of which breaks into volleying spray
a-top and rattles down like hailstones on the
fore-deck.

But next day the wind has hauled ahead, and
she has to make her way by tacking. She loses
as little as possible on her zigzag course by
sailing close to the wind, that is, by pointing
as nearly into it as she can while still ' keeping
a full on ' every working sail. Presently the
skipper, having gone as far to one side of his
straight course as he thinks proper, gives the
caution ; whereupon the braces are taken off
the pins and coiled down on deck, all clear for
running, while the spanker-boom is hauled in
amidships so that the spanker may feel the
wind and press the stern a-lee, which helps the
bow to windward. Then the ' old man ' (called

so whatever his age may be) sings out at the top of his voice, 'Ready, oh!' The helm is eased down on his signal, so as not to lose way suddenly. When it is quite down he shouts again, 'Helm's a-lee!' on which the fore and head sheets (holding the sails attached to the foremast and bowsprit) are let go and over-hauled. The vessel swings round, the spanker pressing her stern in one direction and the sails at the bows offering very little resistance now their sheets are let go. The skipper's eye is on the mainsail, which is the point of pivoting. Directly the wind is out of it and it begins to shiver he yells, 'Raise tacks and sheets!' when, except that the foretack is held a bit to prevent the foresail from bellying aback, all the remaining ropes that held the ship on her old tack are loosed. A roar of wind-waves rushes through the sails, and a tremor runs through the whole ship from stem to stern. The skipper waits for the first decided breath on her new tack and then shouts, 'Mainsail haul!' when the yards come swinging round so quickly that the men can hardly take in the slack of the braces fast enough. The scene of orderly confusion is now at its height. Every one hauling sings out at the very top of his pipes. The sails are struggling to find their

new set home; while the headsheets forward
thrash about like mad and thump their blocks
against the deck with force enough to dash
your brains out.

Mates and boatswain work furiously, for
the skipper's eye is searching everywhere, and
the skipper's angry words cut the delinquent
like the lash of a well-aimed whip. The boatswain forward has the worst of it, for the restive
sheets and headsails won't come to trim without
a fight when it's breezing up and seas are
running. But presently all the yards get
rightly trimmed, tacks boarded, and bowlines
hauled out taut. She's on a bowline taut
enough to please the old man now; that is, the
ropes leading forward from the middle of the
forward edge of every square sail are so straight
that she is sailing as near the wind as she
can go and keep a full on. 'Go below, the
watch!' and the men off duty tramp down,
the cook and boatswain with their 'oilies'
streaming from their scuffle with the flying
spray and slapping dollops at the bows.

When a quartering trade wind is picked up
sailing is at its easiest; for a well-balanced
suit of canvas will keep her bowling along night
and day with just the lightest of touches at the
wheel. Then is the time to bend her old sails

on; for, unlike a man, a ship puts on her old
suit for fair weather and her new suit for foul.
Then, too, is the time for dog-watch yarning,
when pipes are lit without any fear of their
having to be crammed half-smoked into the
nearest pocket because all hands are called.
Landsmen generally think that most watches
aboard a wind-jammer are passed in yarns and
smoking. But this is far from being the case.
The mates and skipper keep everybody busy
with the hundred-and-one things required to
keep a vessel shipshape : painting, graining,
brightening, overhauling the weak spots in
the rigging, working the ' bear ' to clean the
deck with fine wet sand, helping whomever is
acting as ' Chips ' the carpenter, or the equally
busy ' Sails ' ; or ' doing Peggy ' for ' Slush '
the cook, who much prefers wet grub to dry,
slumgullion coffee to any kind of tea, ready-
made hard bread to ship-baked soft, and any
kind of stodge to the toothsome delights of
dandyfunk and crackerhash. And all this is
extra to the regular routine, with its lamp-
lockers, binnacles, timekeeping, incessant
look-out, and trick at the wheel. Besides,
every man has to look after his own kit, which
he has to buy with his own money, and his
quarters, for which he alone is responsible.

So there is never much time to spare, with watch and watch about, all through the voyage; especially when all the ills that badly fed flesh is heir to on board a deepwaterman incapacitate some hands, while falls from aloft and various accidents knock out others.

The skipper, boatswain, cook, steward, Chips, and Sails keep no watches, and hence are called 'the idlers,' a most misleading term, for they work a good deal harder than their counterparts ashore; though the mates and seamen often work harder still. There are seven watches in a day, reckoned from noon to noon: five of four hours each and two of two hours each. These two, the dog watches, are from four to six and six to eight each afternoon. The crew are divided into port and starboard watches, each under a mate. In Bluenose vessels the port watch was always called by the old name of larboard watch till only the other day. The starboard and larboard got their names because the starboard was the side on which the steering oar was hung before the rudder was invented, and the larboard was the side where the lading or cargo came in.

Bluenoses have no use for nippers, as Britishers call apprentices. But if they had,

and the reader was a green one, he would just
about begin to know the ropes and find his sea
legs by the time that our *Victoria* had run her
southing down to within another day's sail of
the foul-weather zone in the roaring forties
round the Horn, which seamen call ' Old
Stiff.'   Sails are shifted again, and the best new
suit is bent ; for the coming gales have a clear
sweep from the Antarctic to the stormiest coast
of all America, and the enormous, grey-backed
Cape Horners are the biggest seas in the world.

The best helmsmen are on duty now.   Not
even every Bluenose can steer, any more than
every Englishman can box or every Frenchman fence.   There are a dozen different ways
of mishandling a vessel under sail.   Let your
attention wander, and she 'll run up into the
wind and perhaps get in irons, so that she won't
cast either way.   Let her fall off when you 're
running free, and she 'll broach to and get
taken aback.   Or simply let her yaw about
a bit instead of holding true, and you 'll lose a
knot or two an hour.   But do none of these
careless things, observe all the rules as well,
and even then you will never make a helms-
man unless it 's born in you.   Steering is
blown into you by the wind and soaked into
you by the water.   And you must also have

that inborn faculty of touch which tells you
instinctively how to meet a vessel's vagaries—
and no two vessels are alike—as well as how
to make her fall in with all the humours of a
wayward ocean.

The hungry great Antarctic wind comes
swooping down. The *Victoria* lays over to it,
her forefoot slashing, her lee side hissing, the
windward rigging strained and screaming, and
every stitch of canvas drawing full. Still the
skipper carries on. He and his vessel have a
name to keep up ; and he has carried on till
all was blue ere this, and left more than one
steam kettle panting. Every timber, plank,
mast, yard, and tackle wakes to new life and
thrills in response to the sails. She answers her
helm quickly, eagerly. She rides the gallop-
ing waters now as you ride her. And as she
rises to each fresh wave you also rise, with
the same exultant spring, and take the leap in
your stride.

The wind pipes up : a regular gale is evi-
dently brewing ; and most of the canvas must
come off her now or else she 'll soon be stripped
of it. ' Stand by your royal halliards ! ' yells the
second mate. ' Let go your royal halliards ! '
The royals are down for good. The skysails
have been taken in before. Another tre-

mendous blast lays her far over, and the sea
is a lather of foam to windward. The skipper
comes on deck, takes a quick look round, and
shouts at the full pitch of his lungs: 'All
hands shorten sail!' Up come the other
watch in their oilskins, which they have carefully lashed round their wrists and above their
knees to keep the water out. Taking in sail
is no easy matter now. Every one tails on,
puts his back into it, and joins the chorus of
the hard-breathed chanty. The human voices
sound like fitful screams of seabirds, heard in
wild snatches between the volleying gusts;
while overhead the sails are booming like
artillery, as the spilling lines strain to get the
grip. 'Now then, starboard watch, up with
your sail and give the larboard watch a dressing
down!' *Yo—ho! Yo—hay! Yo—ho—oh!*
Up she goes! A hiss, a crash, a deafening
thud, and a gigantic wave curls overhead and
batters down the toiling men, who hang on for
their lives and struggle for a foothold. 'Up
with you!' yells the mate, directly the tangled
coil of yellow-clad humanity emerges like a half-
drowned rat, 'Up with you, boys, and give her
hell!' *Yo—ho! Yo—hay! Yo—ho—harrhh!*
'Turn that!' 'All fast, sir!' 'Aloft and
roll her up! Now then, starbowlines, show

your spunk ! ' Away they go, the mate dash-
ing ahead ; while the furious seas shoot up
vindictive tongues at them and nearly wash
two men clean off the rigging on a level with
the lower topsails. Out on the swaying yard,
standing on the foot-rope that is strung underneath, they grasp at the hard, wet, struggling
canvas till they can pass the gaskets round
the parts still bellying between the buntlines.
' One hand for the ship and one for yourself '
is the rule aloft. But exceptions are more
plentiful than rules on a day like this. Both
hands must be used, though the sail and foot-
ropes rack your body and try their best to shake
you off. If they succeed, a sickening thud on
deck, or a smothered scream and a half-heard
plopp ! overside would be the end of you.

All hands work like fury, for a full
Antarctic hurricane is on them. This great
South Polar storm has swept a thousand
leagues, almost unchecked, before venting its
utmost rage against the iron coasts all round
the Horn. The South Shetlands have only
served to rouse its temper. Its seas have
grown bigger with every mile from the Pole,
and wilder with every mile towards the Horn.
Now they are so enormous that even the truck
of the tall Yankee clipper staggering along to

leeward cannot be seen except when both ships
are topping the crest. Wherever you look
there seems to be an endless earthquake of
mountainous waves, with spuming volcanoes
of their own, and vast, abysmal craters yawn-
ing from the depths. The *Victoria* begins
to labour. The wind and water seem to be
gaining on her every minute. She groans in
every part of her sorely racked hull; while up
aloft the hurricane roars, rings, and screeches
through the rigging.

But suddenly there is a new and far more
awful sound, which seems to still all others,
as a stupendous mother wave rears its huge,
engulfing bulk astern. On it comes, faster
and higher, its cavernous hollow roaring
and its overtopping crest snarling viciously
as it turns forward, high above the poop.
' Hold on for your lives ! ' shout the mates
and skipper. They are not a moment
too soon. The sails are blanketed, and
the ship seems as if she was actually being
drawn, stern first, into the very jaws of the
sea. A shuddering pause . . . and then, with
a stunning crash, the whole devouring mass
bursts full on deck. The stricken *Victoria* reels
under the terrific shock, and then lies dead
another anxious minute, utterly helpless, her

deck awash with a smother of foaming water,
and her crew apparently drowned. But presently her stern emerges through the dark,
green-grey after-shoulder of the wave. She
responds to the lift of the mighty barrel with a
gallant effort to shake herself free. She rises,
dripping from stem to stern. Her sails refill
and draw her on again. And when the next
wave comes she is just able to take it—but no
more.

The skipper has already decided to heave to
and wait for the storm to blow itself out. But
there is still too much canvas on her. Even
the main lower topsail has to come in. The
courses, or lowest square sails, have all come
in before. The little canvas required for lying
to must neither be too high nor yet too low. If
it is too high, it gives the wind a very dangerous
degree of leverage. If it is too low, it violently
strains the whole vessel by being completely
blanketed when in the trough of the sea and
then suddenly struck full when on the crest.
The main lower topsail is at just the proper
height. But only the fore and mizzen ones
are wanted to balance the pressure aloft. So
in it has to come. And a dangerous bit of work
it gives ; for it has to be hauled up from right
amidships, where the deck is wetter than a

half-tide rock. The yellow-oilskinned crew tail on and heave. *Yo—ho! Yo—hay!* 'Hitch it! Quick, for your lives, hang on, all!' A mountainous wall of black water suddenly leaps up and crashes through the windward rigging. The watch goes down to a man, some hanging on to the rope as if suspended in the middle of a waterfall, for the deck is nearly perpendicular, while others wash off altogether and fetch up with a dazing, underwater thud against the lee side. Inch by inch the men haul in, waist-deep most of the time and often completely under. *Yo—ho! Yo—hay! harrhh,* and they all hold breath till they can get their heads out again. *Yo—ho! Yo—hay!* 'In with her!' *Heigh—o—oh!* 'Turn that!' 'All fast!'

''Way aloft and roll her up quick!' The tossing crests are blown into spindrift against the weather yardarm, while a pelting hailstorm stings the wet, cold hands and faces. The men tear at the sail with their numb fingers till their nails are bleeding. They hit it, pull it, clutch at it for support. Certain death would follow a fall from aloft; for the whole deck is hidden under a surging, seething mass of water. You would swear the water's boiling if it wasn't icy cold. The skipper's at the wheel, watching his chance. There is no such thing as a good chance now. But he sees one of some kind, just as the men get the sail on the yard and are trying to make it fast. Down goes the helm, and her head comes slowly up to the wind. 'She's doing it—— No! Hang on, all! Great snakes, here comes a sea!' Struck full, straight on her beam, by wind and sea together, the *Victoria* lays over as if she would never stop. Over she heels to it—over, over, over! A second is a long suspense at such a time as this. The sea breaks in thunder along her whole length, and pours in a sweeping cataract across her deck, smashing the boats and dragging all loose gear to leeward. Over she heels—over, over, over! The yards are nearly up and down. The men cling desperately, as if to an inverted mast. And well they may, especially on the leeward arm that dips them far under a surge of water which seems likely to snap the whole thing off. But the *Victoria's* cargo and ballast never shift an inch. Her stability is excellent. And as the heaving shoulder eases down she holds her keel in, just before another lurch would send her turning turtle. A pause . . . a quiver . . . and she begins to right. 'Now then,' roars the indomitable mate, the moment his dripping

yardarm comes from under, ' turn to, there—
d' y' think we 're going to hang on here the
whole damn' day ? ' Whereupon the men
turn to again with twice the confidence and
hearty goodwill that any other form of re-
assurance could possibly have given them.

As she comes back towards an even keel the
wind catches the sails. The skipper is still at
the wheel, to which he and the two men whose
trick it is are clinging. ' Hard-a-lee ! ' and
round she goes this time, till she snuggles into
a good lie-to, which keeps her alternately coming up and falling off a little, by the counter-
action of the sails and helm. Here she rides
out the storm, dipping her lee rail under,
climbing the wild, gigantic seas, and working
off her course on the cyclone-driven waters ;
but giving watch and watch about a chance to
rest before she squares away again.

Next morning the skipper hardly puts his
head out before he yells the welcome order
to set the main lower topsail—from the lee
yardarm of which a dozen men had nearly
gone to Davy Jones's locker only yesterday.
He takes a look round ; then orders up reefed
foresail and the three upper topsails, also
reefed. Up goes the watch aloft and lays out
on the yard. ' Ready ? ' comes the shouted

query from the bunt. ' Ay, ay, sir ! ' ' Haul out to windward ! ' *Eh—hai, o—ho, o—ho—oh !* ' Far enough, sir ? ' ' Haul out to leeward ! ' *Eh—hai, o—ho, o—ho—oh !* ' That 'll do ! Tie her up and don't miss any points ! ' ' Right-oh ! Lay down from aloft and set the sail ! ' *Yo—ho, yo—hai, yo—ho—oh !* Then the chanty rises from the swaying men, rises and falls, in wavering bursts of sound, as if the gale was whirling it about :

> Blow the man down, blow the man down,
> 'Way-ho ! Blow the man down.
> Blow the man down from Liverpool town ;
> Give us some wind to blow the man down.

And so the gallant ship goes outward-bound ; and homeward-bound the same. At last she 's back in Halifax, after a series of adventures that would set an ordinary lands-man up for life. But the only thing the Nova Scotian papers say of her is this : ' Arrived from sea with general cargo—ship *Victoria,* John Smith, master, ninety days from Val-paraiso. All well.'

No mention of that terrible Antarctic hurri-cane ? No ' heroes ' ? No heroics ?

It 's all in the day's work there.

CHAPTER VIII

STEAMERS

STEAMERS and all other machine-driven craft are of very much greater importance to Canada now than canoes and sailing craft together. But their story can be told in a chapter no longer than the one devoted to canoes alone; and this for several reasons. The tale of the canoe begins somewhere in the immemorial past and is still being told to-day. The story of the sailing ship is not so old as this. But it is as old as the history of Canada. It is inseparably connected with Canada's fortunes in peace and war. It is Canada's best sea story of the recent past. And, to a far greater extent than the tale of the canoe, it is also a story of the present and the immediate future. Moreover, sailing craft helped to make turning points of Canadian history as only a single steamer ever has. Sailing craft made Canada known distinctively among every great seafaring people as steamers never have,

And while the building, ownership, and actual
navigation of sailing craft once made Canada
fourth among the shipping countries of the
world, the change to steam and steel, coinciding
with the destruction of the handiest timber
and the development of inland forms of business, put no less than eight successful rivals
ahead of her.

Every one knows that James Watt turned
the power of steam to practical use in the
eighteenth century. But it was not till the
first year of the nineteenth that a really work-
able steamer appeared, though the British,
French, and Americans had been experimenting for years, just as ingenious men had been
experimenting with stationary engines long
before Watt. This pioneer steamer was the
Charlotte Dundas, which ran on the Forth
and Clyde Canal in Scotland in 1801. Six
years later Fulton's *Clermont*, engined by the
British firm of Boulton and Watt, ran on
the Hudson from New York to Albany. Two
years later again the *Accommodation*, the first
steamer in Canada, was launched at Montreal,
and engined there as well. She was built for
John Molson by John Bruce, a shipbuilder,

and John Jackson, an engineer. She was eighty-five feet over all and sixteen feet in the beam. Her engine was six horse-power, and her trial speed five knots an hour. She was launched, broadside on, behind the old Molson brewery. She was fitted up for twenty passengers, but only ten went on her maiden trip. The fare was eight dollars down to Quebec and ten dollars back. The following is interesting as a newspaper account of the first trip made by the first Canadian steamer. It is taken, word for word, from an original copy of the *Quebec Gazette* of November 9, 1809.

The Steam Boat, which was built at Montreal last winter, arrived here on Saturday last, being her first trip. She was 66 hours on the passage, of which she was at anchor 30. So that 36 hours is the time which, in her present state, she takes to come down from Montreal to Quebec [over 160 statute miles]. On Sunday last she went up against wind and tide from Bréhault's wharf to Lymburner's ; but her progress was very slow. It is obvious that her machinery, at present, has not sufficient force for this River. But there can be no doubt of the possibility of

perfectioning it so as to answer every
purpose for which she was intended; and
it would be a public loss should the pro-
prietors be discouraged from persevering
in their undertaking.

They did not fail to persevere. When Molson
found that ox-teams were required to tow her
up St Mary's Current, below Montreal, he
ordered a better engine of thirty horse-power
from Boulton and Watt in England, and put
it into the *Swiftsure* in 1811. This steamer was
twice the size of the *Accommodation*, being 120
by 24 feet; and the *Quebec Gazette* waxed
eloquent about her:

The Steam Boat arrived here from
Montreal on Sunday. She started from
Montreal at 5 o'clock on Saturday morning,
and anchored at Three Rivers, which she
left on Sunday morning at 5 o'clock, and
arrived at the King's Wharf, Quebec, at
half-past two; being only 24 hours and
a half under way between the two cities,
with a strong head wind all the way. She
is most superbly fitted up, and offers
accommodation for passengers in every
respect equal to the best hotel in Canada.
In short, for celerity and security, she well

deserves the name of *Swiftsure*. America cannot boast of a more useful and expensive undertaking by one individual, than this of Mr Molson's. His Excellency, the Governor-in-chief, set out for Montreal on Tuesday afternoon, in the Steam Boat.

The following letter from Molson, for the information of Sir George Prevost, governor-general during the War of 1812, refers to one of the first tenders ever made, in any part of the world, to supply steamer transport for either naval or military purposes. It was received at Quebec by Commissary-General Robinson on February 6, 1813 :

I received a letter from the Military Secretary, under date of the 15th Decr. last, informing me of His Excellency's approval of a Tender I had made of the Steam Boat for the use of Government ; wherein I am likewise informed that you would receive instructions to cause an arrangement to be made for her Service during the ensuing Season. For the Transport of Troops and conveyance of light Stores, it will be necessary to fit her up in a manner so as to be best adapted for the purpose, which will be in my opinion something after the mode of a Transport. For a passage Boat she would have to be fitted up quite in a different manner. If you wish her to be arranged in any particular manner under the direction of any Person, I am agreeable. I should be glad to be informed if His Excellency wishes or expects that I shall sail in her myself, whether Government or I furnish the Officers and men to Navigate and Pilot her, the Engineer excepted, the fuel and all other necessarys that may be required for her use. I imagine the arrangement must be for the Season, not by the Trip, as Government may wish to detain her for particular purposes. Ensurance I do not believe can be effected for less than 30 p. cent for the Season, therefore I must take the risque upon myself.

Within five years of this tender Molson's St Lawrence Steamboat Company had six more steamers running. In 1823 a towboat company was formed, and the *Hercules* towed the *Margaret* from Quebec to Montreal. The well-known word ' tug ' was soon brought into use from England, where it originated from the fact that the first towboat in the world was called *The Tug*. In 1836, before the first steam railway train ran from La Prairie to St Johns, the Torrance Line, in opposition to the Molson Line, was running the *Canada*, which was then the largest and fastest steamer in the whole New World. Meanwhile steam navigation had been practised on the Great Lakes for twenty years; for in 1817 the little *Ontario* and the big *Frontenac* made their first trips from Kingston to York (now Toronto). The *Frontenac* was built at Finkles Point, Ernestown, eighteen miles from Kingston, by Henry Teabout, an American who had been employed in the shipyards of Sackett's Harbour at the time of the abortive British attack in 1813. She was about seven hundred tons, schooner rigged, engined by Boulton and Watt, and built at a total cost of $135,000. A local paper said that ' her proportions strike the eye very agreeably, and good judges have pronounced this to be the best piece of naval architecture of the kind yet produced in America.'

Canals and steamers naturally served each other's turn. There was a great deal of canal building in the twenties. The Lachine Canal, opening up direct communication west of Montreal, was dug out by 1825, the Welland, across the Niagara peninsula, by 1829, and the

Rideau, near Ottawa, by 1832. A few very small canals had preceded these ; others were to follow them ; and they were themselves in their infancy of size and usefulness. But the beginning had been made.

The early Canadian steamers and canals did credit to a poor and thinly peopled country. But none of them ranked as a pioneering achievement in the world at large. This kind of achievement was reserved for the *Royal William,* a vessel of such distinction in the history of shipping that her career must be followed out in detail.

She was the first of all sea-going steamers, the first that ever crossed an ocean entirely under steam, and the first that ever fired a shot in action. But her claims and the spurious counter-claims against her must both be made quite clear. She was not the first steamer that ever put out to sea, for the Yankee *Phœnix* made the little coasting trip from Hoboken to Philadelphia in 1809. She was not the first steamer in Canadian salt water, for the *St John* crossed the Bay of Fundy in 1826. And she was not the first vessel with a steam engine that crossed an ocean, for the Yankee *Savannah* crossed from Savannah to Liverpool in 1819. The

TRANSPORT *BECKWITH* AND BATEAUX, LAKE ONTARIO, 1816

From the John Ross Robertson Collection, Toronto Public Library

Phœnix and *St John* call for no explanation. The *Savannah* does, especially in view of the claims so freely made and allowed for her as being the first regular steamer to cross an ocean. To begin with, she was not a regular sea-going steamer with auxiliary sails like the *Royal William*, but a so-called clipper-built, full-rigged ship of three hundred tons with a small auxiliary engine and paddle-wheels made to be let down her sides when the wind failed. She did not even steam against head winds, but tacked. She took a month to make Liverpool, and she used steam for only eighty hours altogether. She could not, indeed, have done much more, because she carried only seventy-five tons of coal and twenty-five cords of wood, and she made port with plenty of fuel left. Her original log (the official record every vessel keeps) disproves the whole case mistakenly made out for her by some far too zealous advocates.

The claims of the *Royal William* are proved by ample contemporary evidence, as well as by the subsequent statements of her master, John M‘Dougall, her builder, James Goudie, and John Henry, the Quebec founder who made some castings for her engines the year after they had been put into her at Montreal.

M'Dougall was a seaman of indomitable perseverance, as his famous voyage to England shows. Goudie, though only twenty-one, was a most capable naval architect, born in Canada and taught his profession in Scotland. His father was a naval architect before him and had built several British vessels on the Great Lakes for service against the Americans during the War of 1812. Both Goudie and Henry lived to retell their tale in 1891, when the Canadian government put up a tablet to commemorate what pioneering work the *Royal William* had done, both for the inter-colonial and inter-imperial connection.

The first stimulus to move the promoters of the *Royal William* was the subsidy of $12,000 offered by the government of Lower Canada in 1830 to the owners of any steamer over five hundred tons that would ply between Quebec and Halifax. Half this amount had been offered in 1825, but the inducement was not then sufficient. The Quebec and Halifax Navigation Company was formed by the leading merchants of Quebec joined with a few in Halifax. The latter included the three Cunard brothers, whose family name has been a household word in transatlantic shipping circles from that day to this. On September 2,

1830, Goudie laid the keel of the *Royal William* in the yard belonging to George Black, a shipbuilder, and his partner, John Saxton Campbell, formerly an officer in the 99th Foot, and at this time a merchant and shipowner in Quebec. The shipyard was situated at Cape Cove beside the St Lawrence, a mile above the citadel, and directly in line with the spot on which Wolfe breathed his last after the Battle of the Plains.

The launch took place on Friday afternoon, April 29, 1831. Even if all the people present had then foreknown the *Royal William's* career they could not have done more to mark the occasion as one of truly national significance. The leaders among them certainly looked forward to some great results at home. Quebec was the capital of Lower Canada; and every Canadian statesman hoped that the new steamer would become a bond of union between the three different parts of the country—the old French province by the St Lawrence, the old British provinces down by the sea, and the new British province up by the Lakes.

The mayor of Quebec proclaimed a public holiday, which brought out such a concourse of shipwrights and other shipping experts as hardly any other city in the world could show.

Lord Aylmer was there as governor-general to represent King William IV, after whom the vessel was to be named the *Royal William* by Lady Aylmer. This was most appropriate, as the sailor king had been the first member of any royal house to set foot on Canadian soil, which he did at Quebec in 1787, as an officer in H.M.S. *Pegasus*. The guard and band from the 32nd Foot were drawn up near the slip. The gunners of the Royal Artillery were waiting to fire the salute from the new citadel, which, with the walls, was nearing completion, after the Imperial government had spent thirty-five million dollars in carrying out the plans approved by Wellington. Lady Aylmer took the bottle of wine, which was wreathed in a garland of flowers, and, throwing it against the bows, pronounced the historic formula: 'God bless the *Royal William* and all who sail in her.' Then, amid the crash of arms and music, the roaring of artillery, and the enthusiastic cheers of all the people, the stately vessel took the water, to begin a career the like of which no other Canadian vessel ever equalled before that time or since.

Her engines, which developed more than two hundred horse-power, were made by Bennett and Henderson in Montreal and sent to meet

THE *ROYAL WILLIAM*

From the original painting in possession of the Literary and Historical Society of Quebec

her a few miles below the city, as the vessel towing her up could not stem St Mary's Current. Her hull was that of a regular sea-going steamer, thoroughly fit to go foreign, and not the hull of an ordinary sailing ship, like the *Savannah*, with paddles hung over the sides in a calm. Goudie's master, Simmons of Greenock, had built four steamers to cross the Irish Sea; and Goudie probably followed his master's practice when he gave the *Royal William* two deep 'scoops' to receive the paddle-boxes nearer the bows than the stern. The tonnage by builder's measurement was 1370, though by net capacity of burden only 363. The length over all was 176 feet, on the keel 146. Including the paddle-boxes the breadth was 44 feet; and, as each box was 8 feet broad, there were 28 feet clear between them. The depth of hold was 17 feet 9 inches, the draught 14 feet. The rig was that of a three-masted topsail schooner. There were fifty passenger berths and a good saloon.

The three trips between Quebec and Halifax in 1831 were most successful. But 1832 was the year of the great cholera, especially in Quebec, and the *Royal William* was so harassed by quarantine that she had to be laid up there. The losses of that disastrous season

decided her owners to sell out next spring for
less than a third of her original cost. She was
then degraded for a time into a local tug or
sometimes an excursion boat. But presently
she was sent down to Boston, where the band
at Fort Independence played her in to the tune
of ' God Save the King,' because she was the
first of all steamers to enter a seaport of the
United States under the Union Jack.

Ill luck pursued her new owners, who, on
her return to Quebec, decided to send her
to England for sale. She left Quebec on
August 5, 1833, coaled at Pictou, which lies
on the Gulf side of Nova Scotia, and took
her departure from there on the 18th, for her
epoch-making voyage, with the following most
prosaic clearance: '*Royal William*, 363 tons.
36 men. John M'Dougall, master. Bound to
London. British. Cargo: 254 chaldrons of
coals [nearly 300 tons], a box of stuffed birds,
and six spars, produce of this province. One
box and one trunk, household furniture and a
harp, all British, and seven passengers.' The
fare was fixed at £20, ' not including wines.'

The voyage soon became eventful. Nearly
three hundred tons of coal was a heavy con-
centrated cargo for the tremendous storm she
encountered on the Grand Banks of Newfound-

land. She strained ; her starboard engine was disabled ; she began to leak ; and the engineer came up to tell M'Dougall she was sinking. But M'Dougall held his course, started the pumps, and kept her under way for a week with only the port engine going. The whole passage from Pictou, counting the time she was detained at Cowes repairing boilers, took twenty-five days. M'Dougall, a sturdy Scotsman, native of Oban, must have been sorely tempted to ' put the kettle off the boil ' and run her under sail. But either the port or starboard engine, or both, worked her the whole way over, and thus for ever established her claim to priority in transatlantic navigation under steam alone.

In London she was sold for £10,000, just twice what she had fetched at sheriff's sale in Quebec some months before. She was at once chartered, crew and all, by the Portuguese government, who declined to buy her for conversion into a man-of-war. In 1834, however, she did become a man-of-war, this time under the Spanish flag, though flying the broad pennant of Commodore Henry, who was then commanding the British Auxiliary Steam Squadron against the Carlists in the north of Spain. Two years later, on May 5, 1836, under

her Spanish name of *Isabella Segunda*, she
made another record. When the British
Legion, under Sir de Lacy Evans, was attack-
ing the Carlists in the bay of St Sebastian, she
stood in towards the Carlist flank and there-
upon fired the first shot that any steam man-of-
war had ever fired in action.

Strangely enough, she cannot be said to
have come to any definite end as an individual
ship. She continued in the Spanish service
till 1840, when she was sent to Bordeaux for
repairs. The Spaniards, who are notorious
slovens at keeping things shipshape, had
allowed her to run down to bare rot after her
Britisher-Canadian crew had left her. So the
French bought her for a hulk and left her
where she was. But the Spaniards took her
engines out and put them into a new *Isabella
Segunda*, which was wrecked in a storm on the
Algerian coast in 1860.

Her career of record-making is well worth a
general summary : the *Royal William* was the
first steamer built to foster inter-colonial trade
in Canada ; the first Canadian steamer specially
designed for work at sea; the first sea-going
steamer to enter a port in the United States
under the British flag; the first steam transport
in Portugal ; the first steam man-of-war in

Spain; the first naval steamer that ever fired
a shot in action; and the first vessel in the
world that ever crossed an ocean under steam
alone.

The next step in the history of Canadian
steamers is not concerned with a ship but with
a man, Sir Hugh Allan, who, though the
greatest, was not the first of the pioneers.
The Cunard brothers preceded the Allan
brothers in establishing a transatlantic line.
Samuel Cunard had been one of the share-
holders in the *Royal William*. He had wonderful powers of organization. He knew the
shipping trade as very few have ever known
it; and his name has long since become
historical in this connection. The first
'Cunarder' to arrive in Canada was the
Britannia, 1154 tons, built on the Clyde, and
engined there by Napier. From that time on
till Confederation, that is, from 1840 to 1867,
Cunarders ran from Liverpool to Halifax.
But Halifax was always treated as a port of
call. The American ports were the real
destination. And after 1867 the Cunarders
became practically an Anglo-American, not
an Anglo-Canadian, line. During their connection with Canada, partially renewed in the
present century, the Cunards never did any-

thing really original. They were not among
the first to make the change from wood to
iron or from paddle-wheels to screws. But
they did business honestly and well and always
took care of their passengers' safety.

The Cunards were Canadians. Sir Hugh
Allan was a Scotsman. But he and the line
he founded are unchallengeably first in their
services to Canada. Hugh Allan was born in
1810, the son of a Scottish master mariner who
about that time was mate of a transport carrying supplies to the British Army in the Pen-
insular War. He arrived in Canada when he
was only fifteen, entered the employ of a
Montreal shipping firm when he came of age,
and at forty-eight obtained complete control
of it with his brother Andrew. From that day
to this the Allan family have been the acknowledged leaders of Canadian transatlantic
shipping.

Hugh Allan was a man of boundless energy,
iron will, and consummate business ability.
The political troubles of the Pacific Scandal in
1873 prevented him from anticipating the
present Canadian Pacific Railway in making a
single united service of trains and steamers to
connect England with China and both with
Canada. But what he did succeed in carrying

through, against long odds, was quite enough
for one distinguished business lifetime. He
began by running a line of sailing craft between
Montreal and the mother country in conjunction with his father's firm in Glasgow.
Then, in 1853, he and his brother headed a
company which ordered two iron screw
steamers to be built in Scotland for the St
Lawrence. The first of these, the *Canadian*,
came out to Quebec on her maiden voyage in
1854 ; but both she and her sister ship were
soon diverted to the Crimea, where high rates
were being paid for transports during the war.

In 1858 the Allans contracted with the
government for a weekly mail service and
bought out all their partners, as they alone
considered that the time had come for such a
venture. The subsidy was doubled the next
year to prevent the collapse of the service after
a widespread financial panic. But heavy for-
feits were imposed for lateness in delivering
mails, an adverse factor in the greatest fight
against misfortune ever known to Canadian
shipping history. Within eight years the
Allans lost as many vessels. In every case
there was disastrous loss of property ; in some,
a total loss of everything—vessel, cargo, crew,
and passengers.

No other firm has ever had to face such a storm of persistent adversity. But the indomitable Allans emerged triumphant ; and by the time of Confederation, in 1867, the worst was over. Thenceforth they were first in all respects till very recently. In the introduction of shipbuilding improvements they are without a rival still. Their *Bavarian* was the first Atlantic liner entirely built of steel ; their *Parisian* the first to be fitted with bilge keels ; their *Virginian* and *Victorian* the first to use the turbine.

There are only two other salient features of Canadian steamer history that can be mentioned beside the *Royal William* and the Allans : the Richelieu and Ontario Navigation Company and the Canadian Pacific Railway's merchant fleet. True, neither of these comes into quite the same class. The *Royal William* occupies an absolutely unique position in the world at large. The Allans are more intimately connected with the history of Canadian shipping than any other family or firm. Both the *Royal William* and the Allans are landmarks. But the Richelieu and Ontario Navigation Company and the Canadian Pacific Railway Company have also shown abundant energy turned to effective national account.

The Richelieu Steamboat Company was

formed in 1845, and took its other title thirty
years later, when it made its first great
'merger.' It began in a very humble way,
by running two little market boats between
Sorel and Montreal. From the first it had to
fight for its commercial life. The train was
beginning to be a formidable competitor. But
the fight to a finish was the fight of boat against
boat. Fares were cut and cut again. At last
the passengers were offered bed, board, and
transportation for the price of a single meal.
Every day there was a desperate race on the
water. The rival steamers shook and panted
in their self-destroying zeal to be the first to
get the gangway down. Clouds of fire-
streaked smoke poured from their funnels.
More than once a cargo that would burn well
was thrown into the furnaces to keep the steam
up. The public became quite as keen as any
of the crews or companies, and worked ex-
citement up to fever pitch by crowding the
wharves to gamble madly on this daily river
Derby. The stress was too much for the
weaker companies. One by one they either
fell out or 'merged in.' After the merger with
the Ontario Company in 1875 things went on,
with many ups and downs, more in the usual
way of competition. Finally, in 1913, a

general 'pooling merger' was effected by
which practically all Canadian lines came under
one control, from the lower Great Lakes, down
the St Lawrence, through the Gulf, and south
away to the West Indies.   The title of this new
merger is the Canada Steamship Lines Limited.

The Canadian Pacific Railway Company
has half a dozen different fleets at work : one
on the Atlantic, another as a trans-Pacific
line, a third on the Pacific coast, a fourth on
the lakes of British Columbia, a fifth on the
upper Great Lakes, and a sixth as ferries for its
trains.   Thus, by taking the upper Great Lakes
and the West, it divides the trans-Canadian
waters with the Canada Steamship Lines, which
latter take the lower Great Lakes and the East.
A company whose annual receipts and expendi-
ture are balanced at not far short of two
hundred millions of dollars might well seem to
be all-important in every way, especially when
its shipping tonnage exceeds that of the Allans
by over thirty thousand.   But this Chronicle
is a history of at least four hundred years ;
while the famous ' C.P.R.' has not as yet been
either forty years a railway line or twenty years
a shipping firm.   There is only one great C.P.R.
disaster to record.   But that is of appalling
magnitude.   Over a thousand lives were lost

when the Norwegian collier *Storstad* sank the *Empress of Ireland* off Rimouski in 1914.

The five principal features of Canadian steamship history have now been pointed out: John Molson's pioneer boats, the *Royal William*, the Allan line, the 'R. and O.' (now the Canada Steamship Lines), and the 'C.P.R.' No other individual feature has any noteworthy Canadian peculiarities. Nor does the general evolution of steam navigation in or around Canada differ notably, in other respects, from the same evolution elsewhere. Steamers have adapted themselves to circumstances in Canada very much as they have in other countries, pushing their persistent way step by step into all the navigable waters, fresh or salt. The Canadian waters, especially the fresh waters, certainly have some marked characteristics of their own, but the steamers have acquired no special character in consequence.

Both Canadian and visiting steamers have always had their duplicates on many other oceans, lakes, and rivers. There is the ubiquitous tug; stubby, noisy, self-assertive, small; but, in its several varieties, the handiest all-

round little craft afloat. It is worth noting
that in the special class of sea tugs the Dutch,
and not the British, are easily first : a curious
exception to the general rule of British supremacy at sea. Then, with many variations and
several intermediate types, there are the two
main distinctive kinds of inland vessels : the
long, low, grimy, cargo-carrying whale-back,
tankship, barge, or other useful form of
ugliness, simply meant to nose her way
through quite safe waters with the utmost
bulk her huge stuffed maw will hold ; and, at
the opposite end of the scale, the high, white,
gaily decorated ' palace ' steamer, with tier
upon tier of decks, and a strong suggestion of
the theatre all through. Sea-going craft show
the same variations within a given type and the
same intermediate types between the two ends
of the scale. But the general distinction is
quite as well marked, though the necessity for
seaworthy hulls brings about a closer resem-
blance along the water-line. There is the cargo
boat, long, comparatively low, and rather
dingy ; with derricks and vast holds, which
remind one of the tentacles and stomach of an
octopus. The opposite extreme is the great
passenger liner, much larger and more shapely
in the hull ; but best distinguished, at any

distance, by her towering, white, super-structural decks, with their clean-run symmetry fore and aft.

The ' Britisher ' is the predominant type in Canadian waters. This is natural enough, considering that the British Isles build nearly all ' Britishers,' most ' Canadians,' and many foreigners, and that the tonnage actually under construction there in 1913 exceeded the total tonnage owned by any other country except Germany and the United States, while it greatly exceeded the total tonnage under construction in all other countries of the world put together, including Germany and the United States. The British practice is naturally the prevailing one both in shipbuilding and marine engineering. But there is a general conformity to certain leading ideas everywhere. The engine is passing out of the stage in which the fuel-made steam worked machinery, which, in its turn, worked propellers ; and passing into the stage in which the latent forces of the fuel itself are brought to bear more directly on propellers, that is to say, into the stage of internal combustion engines and the turbine-driven screw. The hull has changed more and more in its proportions between length and breadth since the supplanting of wood by steel.

Instead of a length equal at most to five beams there are lengths of more than ten beams now. This means a radical change in framing. The old wooden vessel, as we have seen, had a frame looking like the skeleton of a man's body, with the keel for a backbone and multitudinous ribs at right angles to it. But the new steel vessel, especially if built on the excellent Isherwood principle, looks entirely different. The transverse ribs are there, of course, but in a modified form. They do not catch the eye, which now, instead of being drawn from side to side, is led along from end to end by what looks like, and really is, a complete ribbing of internal keels. The whole system has, in fact, been changed from the transverse to the longitudinal.

The subject is well worth pursuing for its own sake. But the modern developments of naval architecture and waterborne trade which Canada shares with the rest of the world do not concern us any further here.

CHAPTER IX

FISHERIES

THE fisheries of Canada are the most important
in the world. True as this statement is, it
needs some explanation. In the first place,
Newfoundland is included, in accordance with
its inclusion under all other headings in this
book. Then, all the wholly or partly unexploited waters are taken into consideration,
including Hudson Bay and the Arctic ocean.
And, thirdly, the catch made by foreigners in
all waters neighbouring the Canadian coasts
is not left out. Thus the Canadian fisheries
are held to mean all the fisheries, fresh and salt,
in or nearest to the whole of British North
America. This is a perfectly fair basis to
start from. It is, indeed, the fairest basis that
can be found, as it affords a fixed territorial
standard of comparison with other countries;
and standards of comparison are particularly
hard to fix in regard to fishing. French and
Americans fish round Newfoundland, in waters

closely neighbouring British territory and far removed from their own ; and the fishing fleets of the British Isles work grounds as far asunder as the White Sea is from Africa. Yet all their catches figure in official reports as being French, American, or British. And so they legally are, if the men who make them observe the three-mile open-water distance-limit fixed by international agreement as the proper territorial boundary of government control. Beyond three miles from shore all ' nationals ' are on an equal footing.

Now, taking the word Canadian in the sense just defined, it is safe to say that Canadian waters contain a greater quantity of the principal food fishes than those of any other country. The truth of this statement depends on three facts. The first is that practically all fish landed in Canada are caught in Canadian waters. This is a marked contrast to what happens in the other great fishing countries, like the United States, the British islands, Germany, Norway, and France, all of which send some of their fleets very far afield. The second fact is the statistics of totals caught. Canada at present catches fifty million dollars' worth of fish from her own waters in a single year. The ' Britisher ' and ' Yankee ' totals each exceed this, though not by much. But the Yankee total includes a good deal, and the Britisher total a very great deal, caught far outside their own waters. No other country is even worthy of comparison with these. The third fact is that the Canadian total, already advancing more rapidly than any other total, must continue to advance more rapidly still, because Canada has the greatest area of unexploited fish-bearing waters in the world.

If the amount caught per head of the total population is made the standard of comparison, then the Canadian catch is more than five times greater than the Britishers', and more than ten times greater than the Yankees'. And if, still keeping to this standard, the comparison is made between totals caught in strictly territorial waters, Canada surpasses both Britishers and Yankees, put together, ten times over.

There are nearly 120,000 fishermen in Canada and Newfoundland. The proportion in Newfoundland is, of course, by far the higher of the two. About 60,000 people are engaged in handling fish ashore, and many thousands more are concerned in trading with fish products. One way and another, the livelihood of at least one Canadian in every fifteen, and one Newfoundlander in every two, is entirely dependent

on fishing. Statistics are apt to become be-
wildering unless carefully marshalled in tabular
form. But one or two items might be added.
There is a fishing craft of some kind, however
small most of them are, to every single family
in Newfoundland, a proportion immeasurably
higher than in any other country in the world.
But even more astonishing is the statistical fact
that the fishermen of all nations in Newfoundland waters catch each year nearly 1000 codfish for every single individual person there is
in the whole population of the island. After
this, numbers seem rather to weaken than
strengthen the argument. But it is worth
mentioning that there are nearly 80,000 local
fishing boats of all sorts actually counted by
the governments of Canada and Newfoundland,
from little rowboats up to full-powered steamers
of considerable tonnage ; that nearly a quarter
of the whole number in 1913 already had
gasoline or other motors ; that the total length
of all the Canadian and Newfoundland coast-
lines is nearly equal to that of the equator ;
that, excluding all parts of the Great Lakes
within the American sphere of influence, the
fresh-water fishing area of Canada exceeds
the total area of the British Isles by more than
100,000 square miles ; and, finally, that the

mere increase of value in the fisheries of the single province of British Columbia, within a single year, has exceeded the value of the total catch marketed in several of the smaller states of Europe and America.

The two principal salt-water craft that have a history behind them and a sphere of active usefulness to-day are the schooner and its tender, the little dory. A schooner is a fore-and-aft-rigged vessel with at least two masts and four sails—mainsail, foresail, jib, and the staysail generally called a wind-bag. The schooner rig makes the handiest all-round vessel known. It can be managed by fewer hands in proportion to its tonnage than any other, and its sails do the greatest amount of work under the most varied conditions. Other rigs may beat it on special points ; but the general sum of all the sailing virtues is decidedly its own. It takes you more nearly into a head wind than most others, and scuds before a lubber's wind dead aft with a maximum of canvas spread out ' wing-and-wing '—one big sail to port and the other out to starboard.

The dory is a two-man rowboat which possesses as many of the different, and some-times contradictory, good points of the canoe, skiff, punt, and lifeboat as it is possible to

combine in a single craft. It can be rowed,
sculled, sailed, or driven by a motor. It is the
first aquatic plaything for the boys, and often
the last salvation for the men. The way it
will ride out a storm that makes a liner labour
and sinks any ill-found vessel like a stone is
little short of marvellous. It has a flattish
bottom, sheering up at both ends, which are
high in the gunwale. The flat stern, which
looks like a narrow wedge with the point cut
off, is a good deal more waterborne than the
bow and rises more readily to the seas without
presenting too much resisting surface to either
wind or wave. Each schooner has several
dories, which fish all round it, thus suggesting
what is often called the hen-and-chickens
style. At dark, or when the catch has filled
the dory, the men come back on board, ' nest-
ing ' half a dozen dories, one inside the other.
But sometimes a sudden storm, especially if it
follows fog, will set the chickens straying ; and
then the men must ride it out moored to some
sort of drogue or floating anchor. The usual
drogue is a trawl tub, quite perfect if filled with
oil-soaked cotton waste to make a ' slick '
which keeps the crests from breaking. The
tub is hove into the water, over the stern, to
which it is made fast by a bit of line long

enough to give the proper scope. And there, with the live ballast of two expert men, whose home has always been the water, the dory will thread its perilous way unharmed through spume and spindrift, across the engulfing valleys and over the riven hill-tops of the sea.

These schooners and their attendant dories have a long and stirring history of their own. But they are not the only craft, nor yet the oldest; and though their history would easily fill a volume twice the size of this, it would only tell us a very little about Canadian fisheries as a whole, from first to last. Even if we went back by hasty steps, of quite a century each, we should never get into the wild days of the early 'fishing admirals' before our space gave out. All we can do here is simply to mention the steps themselves, and then pass on. First, the red men, few in number, and fishing from canoes. Then the early whites, dispossessing the red men and steadily increasing. They came from all seafaring peoples, and had no other form of justice than what could be enforced by 'fishing admirals,' who won their rank by the order of their arrival on the Banks —admiral first, vice-admiral second, rear-admiral third. Then government by men-of-war began, and Newfoundland itself became, officially, a man-of-war, under its own captain from the Royal Navy. Finally, civil self-government followed in the usual way.

All through there was a constantly growing and apparently inextricable entanglement of international complications, which were only settled by The Hague agreement in the present century. And only within almost as recent times has what may be called the natural history of Canadian fisheries begun to follow the inevitable trend of evolution which gradually changes the civilized fisherman from a hunter into a farmer. As man increases in number, and his means of hunting down game increase still faster, a time inevitably comes when he disturbs the balance of nature to such an extent that he must either exterminate his prey or begin to ' farm ' it, that is, begin to breed and protect as well as kill it. Fisheries are no exception to this rule ; and what with close seasons, prohibitions, hatcheries, and other means of keeping up the supply of fish, the fishing population is beginning, though only to a very small extent as yet, to make the change. Some day we shall talk of our pedigree cod, but the men of this generation will not live to see it.

The change is beneficial for the mere mouths

there are to fill. But it means less and less demand for those glorious and most inspiring qualities of courage, strength, and bodily skill which are required by all who pit themselves against Nature in her wildest and most dangerous moods. The fisherman and sealer have only the elements to fight ; though this too often means a fight for life. A hundred men were frozen to death on the ice, and two hundred more were drowned in the Gulf, during the great spring seal hunt blizzard of 1914. Whalemen still occasionally fight for their lives against their prey as well. And all three kinds of deep-sea fishery have bred so many simple-minded heroes that only cowards attract particular attention.

No modern reader needs reminding that whales are not fish but mammals, belonging to the same order of the animal kingdom as monkeys, dogs, and men. They include the most gigantic of all creatures, living or extinct. The enormous 'right' whales of the story-books have been driven far north in greatly diminished numbers. The equally famous sperm whales have always been very rare, as they prefer southern waters. But the 'finners,' which are still fairly common, include the 'sulphurs,' among which there have been specimens far exceeding any authentic sperms or 'rights.' Even the humpbacks and common finbacks, both well known in Canadian waters, occasionally surpass the average size of sperms and 'rights.' But the sulphur is probably the only kind of whale which sometimes grows to a hundred feet and more.

Whaling is done in three different ways: from canoes, from boats sent off by sailing ships, and from steamers direct. The Indians whaled from canoes before the white man came, and a few Indians, Eskimos, and French Canadians are whaling from canoes to-day. Eskimos sometimes attack a large whale in a single canoe, but oftener with a regular flotilla of kayaks, and worry it to death; as the Indians once did with bark canoes in the Gulf and lower St Lawrence. Modern canoe whaling is done from a North-Shore wooden canoe of considerable size and weight with a crew of two men. It is now chiefly carried on by a few French Canadians living along the north shore of the lower St Lawrence. It is not called whaling but porpoise-hunting, from the mistaken idea that the little white whale is a porpoise, instead of the smallest kind of whale, running up to over twenty feet in length. It is dangerous work at best, and a good many men

are drowned. As a rule they are very skilful,
and they nearly always jab carefully while
sitting down. Sometimes, however, the rare
occasion serves the rare harpooner, when the
whale and canoe appear as if about to meet
each other straight head-on. Then, in a
flash, the man in the bow is up on his feet, with
the harpoon so poised that the rocking water,
the mettlesome canoe, and his watchful com-
rade in the stern, all form part of the con-
centrated energy with which he brings his
every faculty to a single point of instantaneous
action. There, for one fateful moment, he
stands erect, his whole tense body like the full-
drawn bow before it speeds the arrow home.
He throws : and then, for some desperate
minutes, it is often a fight to a finish between
the whale's life and his own.

The old wooden whaling vessel under mast
and sail is almost extinct. But it had a long
and splendid career. The Basques, who were
then the models for the world, began in the
Gulf before Jacques Cartier came ; and worked
the St Lawrence with wonderful success as
high as the basin of Quebec. The French
never whaled in Canada; but the ' Bluenose '
Nova Scotians did, and held their own against
all comers. ' A dead whale or a stove boat '

was the motto for every man who joined the
chase. Discipline was stern; and rightly so.
A green hand was allowed one show of funk;
but that was all. However, there was very
little funking so long as Britishers, Bluenoses,
and Yankees could pick their crews from
among the most adventurous of their own
populations.

Hardly had the long-drawn clarion of the
look-out's *B—l—o—w!* sounded aloft than the
boats were lowered from the davits and began
pulling away towards the likeliest spot for a
rise. Two barbed harpoons, always known
as 'irons,' were carried on the same line,
always called the 'warp.' If both could be
used, so much the better, especially as they
were some distance apart on the warp, the
bight of which formed a considerable drag in
the water. Other drags, usually called 'drugs,'
were bits of wood made fast thwart-wise on
the warp, so as to increase the pull on a sound-
ing whale. The coiling and management of
the warp was of the utmost importance.
Many a man has gone to Davy Jones with a
strangling loop of rope around him. Everything, of course, had to be made shipshape in
advance, as there was no time for finishing
touches once the cry of *B—l—o—w!* was

raised. And if there was haste at all times, what was there not when fleets of whalers under different flags were together in the same waters ?

The approach, often made by changing the oars for silent paddles ; the strike ; the flying whale ; the snaking, streaking, zipping line ; the furious tow, with the boat almost leaping from crest to crest ; the long haul in on the gradually slackening warp ; the lancing and the dying flurry, were all exciting enough by themselves. And when a whale showed fight, charged home, and smashed a boat to splinters, it took a smart crew to escape and get rescued in time. A Greenland whale once took fifteen harpoons, drew out six miles of line, and carried down a boat with all hands drowned before it was killed. Old sperms that had once escaped without being badly hurt were always ready to fight again. One fighting whale took down the bow oarsman in its mouth, drowned the next two, and sent the rest flying with a single snap of its jaws. Another fought nine hours, took five harpoons and seven bombs, smashed up three boats, and sank dead—a total loss. A third, after smashing a boat, charged the ship and stove her side so badly that she sank within five minutes.

Yet accidents like these only spurred the whalemen on to greater efforts, not of mere bravado, but of daring skill. Perhaps the most wonderful regular feat of all was 'spading,' which meant slewing the boat close in, as the whale was about to sound, and cutting the tendons of its tremendous death-dealing tail by a slicing blow from the two-handed razor-edged 'spade.' Perhaps the most wonderful of all exceptional escapes was that of a boat which was towed by one whale right over the back of another. And perhaps the most exciting finish to any international race was the one in which the Yankee, who came up second, got 'first iron' by 'pitchpoling' clear over the intervening British boat, whose crew were nearly drowned by this 'slick' Yankee's flying warp.

No wonder old whalemen despise the easier and safer methods of steam whaling practised by the Norwegians in Canadian and other waters at the present day. And yet steam whaling is not without some thrilling risks. The steamers are speedy, handy, small, about one hundred tons or so, with the latest pattern of the explosive harpoon gun originally invented by Sven Foyn in 1880. The range is very short, rarely over fifty yards. The harpoon may be compared to the stick of an

CHAPTER X

ADMINISTRATION

ADMINISTRATION is used here for want of a better general term to cover every form of management that is done ashore, as well as every form of what might be called, by analogy with fleets and armies, non-combatant work afloat. It falls into two natural divisions : the first includes all private management, the second all that concerns the government. Here, even more than in the other chapters, we are face to face with such complex and enormous interests that we can only take the merest glance at what those interests principally are.

The privately managed interests have both their business and their philanthropic sides. Let us take the philanthropic first. Seamen's Institutes have grown from very small beginnings, and are now to be found in every port where English-speaking seamen congregate. They began when, as the saying was, the sailor earnt his money like a horse and spent it like an ass. They flourish when the sailor is much better able to look after himself. But their help is needed still ; and what they have done in the past has not been the least among the influences which have made the common lot of the seaman so very much better than it was. Another excellent influence is that of the Royal National Mission to Deep Sea Fishermen. This mission sends its missioners afloat in its own steamers to tend the sick and bring some of the amenities of shore life within the reach of those afloat. Religion is among its influences, but only in an unsectarian way. Its work in Canadian waters is directed by two able and self-sacrificing men : Dr Grenfell, whose base is at St Anthony's in North-East Newfoundland, and whose beat goes straight down north along the Newfoundland Labrador, which faces the Atlantic ; and Dr Hare, whose base is Harrington, in the centre of the Canadian Labrador, which runs in from the Strait of Belle Isle to Natashquan, more than two hundred miles along the north shore of the Gulf, among a perfect labyrinth of islands.

Next, the business side. As only a single instance can be given, and as ordinary business management in shipping circles more or less resembles what is practised in other commercial affairs, the special factor of marine insurance will alone be taken, as being the most typically maritime and by far the most interesting historically. Ordinary insurance on land is a mere thing of yesterday compared with marine insurance, which, according to some, began in the ancient world, and which was certainly known in the Middle Ages. It is credibly reported to have been in vogue among the Lombards in the twelfth century, and on much the same principles as are followed by Canadians in the twentieth. It was certainly in vogue among the English before Jacques Cartier discovered the St Lawrence. And in 1613, the year Champlain discovered the site of Ottawa, a policy was taken out, in the ordinary course of business, on that famous old London merchantman, the *Tiger*, to which Shakespeare twice alludes, once in *Macbeth* and again in *Twelfth Night*.

Modern practice is based on the Imperial Marine Insurance Act of 1906, which is a development of the Act of 1795, which, in its turn, was a codification of the rules adopted at Lloyd's in 1779. Nothing shows more unmistakably how supreme the British are in every affair of the sea than these striking

facts : that 'A1 at Lloyd's' is an expression
accepted all the world over as a guarantee of
prime efficiency, that nearly every shipping
country in the world has its own imitation of
Lloyd's, nearly always including the name of
Lloyd, and that the original Lloyd's at the Royal
Exchange in London is still unassailably first.
Most people know that Lloyd's originated
from the marine underwriters who used to
meet for both business and entertainment at
Lloyd's coffee-house in the seventeenth century.
But comparatively few seem to know that
Lloyd's, like most of its imitators, is not a
gigantic insurance company, but an association
of carefully selected members, who agree to
carry on their completely independent business
affairs in daily touch with each other. Lloyd's'
method differs from that of ordinary insurance
in being conducted by ' underwriters,' each one
of whom can write his name under any given
risk for any reasonable part of the whole.
Thus, instead of insuring a million with a
company or a single man, the owner lays his
case before Lloyd's, whereupon any members
who choose to do so can sign for whatever
proportion they intend to assume. In this
way individual losses are spread among a
considerable number of underwriters. Long

experience has proved that the individual and associated methods of doing business have nowhere been more happily combined than they are at Lloyd's to-day, and that this special form of combination suits both parties in a shipping risk better than any other known.

Canadian shipping has often resented Lloyd's high rates against the St Lawrence route, and threatened to establish a Lloyd's of its own. Yet, on the whole, the original Lloyd's is the fairest, the soundest, and incomparably the most expert association of its kind the world has ever seen.

Business administration in marine affairs is complex enough. Lloyd's alone is not the subject of one text-book, nor of several, but of a regular and constantly increasing library. What, then, can usefully be said in a very few words about the still more complex affairs of government administration ? The bare enumeration of the duties performed by a single branch of the department of Marine and Fisheries in Canada will give some faint idea of what the whole department does. There are Naval, Fisheries, and Marine branches, each with sub-branches of its own. Among the duties of the Marine branch are the following : the construction of lighthouses and fog-alarms, the maintenance of lights and buoys, the building and maintenance of Dominion steamers, the consideration of all aids to navigation, the maintenance of the St Lawrence ship channel, the weather reports and forecasts, investigations into wrecks, steamboat inspection, cattle-ship inspection, marine hospitals, submarine signals, the carrying out of the Merchant Shipping Act and other laws, humane service, subsidies to wrecking plant, winter navigation, removal of obstructions, examinations for masters' and mates' certificates, control of pilots, government of ports and harbours, navigation of Hudson Bay and northern waters generally, port wardens, wreck receivers, and harbour commissioners.

Besides all this there are, in the work of the department, items like the Dominion registry of more than eight thousand vessels, the administration of the enormous fisheries, and the hydrographic survey. Then, quite distinct from all these Canadian government activities, is the British consular service, maintained by the Imperial government alone, but available for every British subject. And round every-thing, afloat and ashore, supporting, protecting, guaranteeing all, stands the oldest, most glorious, and still the best of all the navies in

the world—the Royal Navy of the mother-
land.

This is only a glance at the conditions of
the present; while each Imperial and Canadian
service, department, branch, and sub-division
has a long, romantic, and most important
history of its own. The lighthouse service
alone could supply hero-tales enough to fill
a book. The weather service is full of absorb-
ing interest. And, what with wireless tele-
graphy, submarine bells, direction indicators,
microthermometers as detectors of ice, and
many other new appliances, the whole practice
of navigation is becoming an equally interesting subject for a book filled with the ' fairy
tales of science.' Even hydrography—that is,
the surveying and mapping (or ' charting ')
of the water—has an appealing interest, to
say nothing of its long and varied history.
Jacques Cartier, though he made no charts,
may be truly called the first Canadian hydrographer; for his sailing directions are admirably clear and correct. In the next century
we find Champlain noting the peculiarities
of the Laurentian waters to good effect; while
in the next again, the eighteenth, we come
upon the famous Captain Cook, one of the
greatest hydrographers of all time. Cook was

at Quebec with Wolfe, and afterwards spent
several years in making a wonderfully accurate
survey of the St Lawrence and Gulf. His pupil,
Vancouver, after whom both a city and an
island have been named, did his work on the
Pacific coast equally well. The principal
hydrographer of the nineteenth century was
Admiral Bayfield, who extended the survey
over the Great Lakes, besides re-surveying all
the older navigational waters with such perfect
skill that wherever nature has not made any
change his work stands to-day, reliable as
ever. And it should be noted that all the
successful official surveys, up to the present
century, were made by naval officers—another
little known and less remembered service done
for Canada by the British guardians of the sea.

CHAPTER XI

NAVIES

THIS is not the place to discuss the naval side of craft and waterways in Canada. That requires a book of its own. But no study of Canada's maritime interests, however short, can close without a passing reference to her naval history.

When the Kirkes, with their tiny flotilla, took Quebec from Champlain's tiny garrison in 1629 the great guiding principles of sea-power were as much at work as when Phips led his American colonists to defeat against Frontenac in 1690, or as when Saunders and Wolfe led the admirably united forces of their enormous fleet and little army to victory in 1759. In the same way the decisive influence of sea-power was triumphantly exerted by Iberville, the French naval hero of Canada, when, with his single ship, the *Pélican*, he defeated his three British opponents in a gallant fight; and so, for the time being, won the

absolute command of Hudson Bay in 1697.
Again, it was naval rather than political and
military forces that made American independence an accomplished fact. The opposition
to the war in England counted for a good deal ;
and the French and American armies for still
more. But the really decisive anti-British
force consisted of practically all the foreign
navies in the world, some—like the French,
Spanish, Dutch, and the Americans' own—
taking an active part in the war, while the
others were kept ready in reserve by the
hostile armed neutrality of Russia, Sweden,
Denmark, Prussia, and the smaller sea-coast
states of Germany. Once again, in the War of
1812, it was the two annihilating American
naval victories on Lakes Erie and Champlain
that turned the scale far enough back to offset
the preponderant British military victories
along the Canadian frontier and prevent the
advance of that frontier beyond Detroit and
into the state of Maine.

There were very few people in 1910 who remembered that the Canadian navy then begun
was the third local force of its kind in Canada,
though the first to be wholly paid and managed
locally. From the launch of La Salle's *Griffon*
in 1679 down to the Cession in 1763 there was

always some sort of French naval force built, manned, and managed in New France, though ultimately paid and directed from royal head-quarters in Paris through the minister of Marine and Colonies. It is significant that 'marine' and 'colonies' were made a single government department throughout the French régime. The change of rule did not entail the abolition of local forces; and from 1755, when a British flotilla of six little vessels was launched on Lake Ontario, down to and beyond the peace with the United States sixty years later, there was what soon became a 'Provincial Marine,' which did good service against the Americans in 1776, when it was largely manned from the Royal Navy, and less good service in 1812, when it was a great deal more local in every way. Two vestiges of those days linger on to the present time, the first in the Canadian Militia Act, which provides for a naval as well as a military militia, permanent forces included, and the second in one of the governor-general's official titles—'Vice-Admiral' of Canada.

The Canadian privateers are even less known than the Provincial Marine. Yet they did a good deal of preying on the enemy at different times, and they amounted altogether to a total which will probably surprise most students of Canadian history. At Halifax alone eighteen Nova Scotian privateers took out letters of marque against the French between 1756 and 1760, twelve more against the French between 1800 and 1805, and no less than forty-four against the Americans during the War of 1812.

The century of peace which followed this war gradually came to be taken so much as a matter of course that Canadians forgot the lessons of the past and ignored the portents of the future. The very supremacy of a navy which protected them for nothing made them forget that without its guardian ships they could not have reached their Canadian nationality at all. Occasionally a threatened crisis would bring home to them some more intimate appreciation of British sea-power. But, for the rest, they took the Navy like the rising and the setting of the sun.

The twentieth century opened on a rapidly changing naval world. British supremacy was no longer to go unchallenged, at least so far as preparation went. The German Emperor followed up his pronouncement, ' Our future is on the sea,' by vigorous action. For the first time in history a German navy became a powerful force, fit to lead, rather than to follow, its Austrian and Italian allies. Also for the first time in history the New World developed a sea-power of first-class importance in the navy of the United States. And, again for the first time in history, the immemorial East produced a navy which annihilated the fleet of a European world-power when Japan beat Russia at Tsu-shima in the centennial year of Nelson at Trafalgar.

These portentous changes finally roused the oversea dominions of the British Empire to some sense of the value of that navy which had been protecting them so efficiently and so long at the mother country's sole expense. But the dawn of naval truth broke slowly and, following the sun, went round from east to west. First it reached New Zealand, then Australia, then South Africa, and then, a long way last, Canada; though Canada was the oldest, the largest, the most highly favoured in population and resources, the richest, and the most expensively protected of them all.

There was a searching of hearts and a gradual comprehension of first principles. Colonies which had been living the sheltered life for generations began to see that their immunity from attack was not due to any warlike virtue of their own, much less to any of their 'victories of peace,' but simply to the fact that the British Navy represented the survival of the fittest in a previous struggle for existence. More than two centuries of repeated struggle, from the Armada in 1588 to Trafalgar in 1805, had given the British Empire a century of armed peace all round the Seven Seas, and its colonies a century's start ahead of every rival. But in 1905 the possible rivals were beginning to draw up once more, thanks to the age-long naval peace; and the launch of her first modern Dreadnought showed that the mother country felt the need of putting forth her strength again to meet a world of new competitors.

The critical question now was whether or not the oversea dominions would do their proper share. They had grown, under free naval protection, into strong commercial nations, with combined populations equal to nearly a third of that in the mother country, and combined revenues exceeding a third of hers. They had a free choice. Canada, for instance, might have declared herself independent, though she could not have made herself more free, and would certainly not have been able to maintain a position of complete independence in any serious crisis. Or she could have destroyed her individual Canadian characteristics by joining the United States; though in this case she would have been obliged to pay her share towards keeping up a navy which was far smaller than the British and much more costly in proportion. As another alternative she could have said that her postal and customs preferences in favour of the mother country, taken in conjunction with what she paid for her militia, were enough. This would have put her far behind New Zealand and Australia, both of whom were doing much more, in proportion to their wealth and population.

There was a very natural curiosity to see what Canada would do, because she was much the senior of the other dominions, while in size, wealth, and population she practically equalled all three of them together. But whatever the expectations were, they were doomed to disappointment, for, while she was last in starting, she did not reach any decisive result at all. Australia, New Zealand—and even South Africa, so lately the scene of a devastating war—each gave money, while Canada gave none. New Zealand, with only one-seventh of Canada's population, gave a Dreadnought, while Canada gave none. Australia had a battle-worthy squadron of her own—but Canada had nothing but a mere flotilla.

The explanation of this strange discrepancy is to be found, partly, in geographical position. The geographical position of Canada differs widely from that of any other dominion. She lives beside the United States, a country with a population ten times greater than her own, a country, moreover, which holds the Monroe Doctrine as an article of faith in foreign policy. This famous doctrine simply means that the United States is determined to be the predominant power in the whole New World and to prevent any outside power from gaining a foothold there. Consequently the United States must defend, if necessary, any weaker nation in America whenever it is attacked by any stronger nation from outside. Of course the United States would exert its power only on its own terms, to which any weaker friend would be obliged to submit. But so long as there was no immediate danger that the public could actually feel, the Monroe Doctrine provided a very handy argument for all those who preferred to do nothing. Another peculiarity of Canada's position is that she is far enough away from the great powers of Europe and from the black and yellow races of Africa and Asia to prevent her from realizing so quickly as the mother country the danger from the first, or so quickly as her sister dominions the danger from the second.

For five successive years, from 1909 to 1913, the naval policy of Canada was the subject of debate in parliament, press, and public meetings. In 1909 the building programme for the German navy brought on a debate in the Imperial parliament which found an echo throughout the Empire. The Canadian parliament then passed a loyal resolution with the consent of both parties. In 1910 these parties began to differ. The Liberals, who were then in power, started a distinctively Canadian navy on a very small scale. In 1911 naval policy was, for the first time, one of the vexed questions in a general election. In 1912 the new Conservative government passed through the House of Commons an act authorizing an appropriation of thirty-five million dollars for three first-class Dreadnought battleships. This happened to be the exact sum paid by the Imperial government for the fortification of Quebec in 1832, and considerably less than one-thirtieth part of what the Imperial government had paid for the naval and military protection of Canada during the British régime. The Senate reversed the decision of the Commons in 1913, with the result that Canada's total naval contribution

up to date consisted of five years' discussion
and a little three-year-old navy which had far
less than half the fighting power of New
Zealand's single Dreadnought.

The two great parliamentary parties agreed
on the general proposition that Canada ought
to do something for her own defence at sea,
and that, within the British Empire, she enjoyed naval advantages which were unobtain-
able elsewhere. But they differed radically on
the vexed question of ways and means. The
Conservatives said there was a naval emergency
and proposed to give three Dreadnoughts to
the Imperial government on certain conditions.
The principal condition was that Canada could
take them back at any time if she wished to use
them for a navy of her own. The Liberals
objected that there was no naval emergency,
and that it was wrong to let any force of any
kind pass out of the control of the Canadian
government. Nothing, of course, could be
done without the consent of parliament; and
the consent of parliament means the consent
of both Houses, the Senate and the Commons
of Canada. There was a Conservative majority
in the Commons and a Liberal majority in the
Senate. The voting went by parties, and a
complete deadlock ensued.

BIBLIOGRAPHICAL NOTE

ALL AFLOAT seems to be the only book of its kind. Not only this, but no other book seems to have been written on the special subject of any one of its eleven chapters. There are many books in which canoes figure largely, but none which gives the history of the canoe in Canada. Books on sailing craft, on steamers, on fisheries, on every aspect of maritime administration, and, most of all, on navies, are very abundant. But, so far, none of them seems to have been devoted exclusively to the Canadian part of these various themes, with the single exception of a purely naval work, *The Logs of the Conquest of Canada*, by the present author, who has consequently been obliged to write a good deal from his own experience with paddle, sail, and steam. Of course there are many excellent articles, some of considerable length, in the Transactions of several learned societies, like the Royal Society of Canada, the Literary and Historical Society of Quebec, the Nova Scotia Historical Society, the Ontario Historical Society, and so on. There are also a certain number of pamphlets and official bluebooks—like those of the department of

Marine and Fisheries; and there is an immense mass of original evidence stored away in the Dominion Archives and elsewhere. But books for the public do not seem to exist; and the suggestion might be hazarded that this whole subject offers one of the best unworked or little-worked fields remaining open to the pioneer in Canadian historical research.

Under these circumstances all that can be done here is to name a few of the many books which either cover some part of the subject incidentally or deal with what is most closely allied to it.

CANOES are mentioned in every book of travel along the inland waterways, kayaks in every book about the Eskimos. La Hontan's *Travels*, though imaginative, give interesting details, as do the much more sober *Travels* of Peter Kalm, the Swedish naturalist. Kohl's *Kitchi-Gami* is a good book. But the list might be extended indefinitely.

SAILING CRAFT and STEAMERS require some sort of nautical dictionary, though even a dictionary sometimes adds to the puzzles of the landsman. Admiral Smyth's *Sailor's Word Book*, and Dana's *Seaman's Friend* (as it is called in the United States), or *Seaman's Manual* (as it is called in England), are excellent. Peake's *Rudimentary Treatise on Shipbuilding* covers the period so well described in Clark's *Clipper Ship Era* and Dana's *Two Years before the Mast*. Sir George Holmes's

Ancient and Modern Ships and Paasch's magnificent polyglot marine dictionary, *From Keel to Truck*, deal with steam as well as sail. Lubbock's *Round the Horn before the Mast* gives a good account of a modern steel wind-jammer. Patton's article on shipping and canals in *Canada and its Provinces* is a very good non-nautical account of its subject, and is quite as long and thorough as the ordinary book. Fry's *History of North Atlantic Steam Navigation* includes a great deal on Canada. *The Times Shipping Number* gives an up-to-date account of British and foreign shipping in 1912. Barnaby's *Naval Development in the Nineteenth Century* is well worth reading. So is Bullen's *Men of the Merchant Service*; and so, it might be added, are a hundred other books.

FISHERIES are the subject of a vast literature. An excellent general account, but more European than Canadian, is Hérubel's *Sea Fisheries*. Grenfell's *Labrador* and Browne's *Where the Fishers Go* give a good idea of the Atlantic coast; so, indeed, does Kipling's *Captains Courageous*. The butchering of seals in the Gulf and round Newfoundland does not seem to have found any special historian, though much has been written on the fur seal question in Alaska. Whaling is recorded in many books. Bullen's *Cruise of the Cachalot* is good reading; but annals that incidentally apply more closely to Bluenose whalers are set forth in Spears's *Story of the New England Whalers*.

Books on the many subjects grouped together under the general title of ADMINISTRATION cannot even be mentioned. Such headings as Marine Insurance, Seamen's Institutes, Lighthouses, Navigation, etc., must be looked up in reference catalogues.

When we come to NAVIES the number of books is so great that they too must be looked up separately. Corbett's *England in the Seven Years' War* and all the works of Admiral Mahan should certainly be consulted. Snider's collection of well-spun yarns, *In the Wake of the Eighteen-Twelvers,* seems to be the only book that has ever been devoted to the old Canadian Provincial Marine.

INDEX

Printed by T. and A. Constable, Printers to His Majesty
at the Edinburgh University Press

CHRONICLES OF CANADA

Edited by George M. Wrong and H. H. Langton of the University of Toronto

A series of thirty-two tersely-written narratives for popular reading, designed to set forth, in historic continuity, the principal events and movements in Canada, from the Earliest Explorers to the Railway Builders.

Chronicles of Canada

* NOTE.—The eight volumes marked with an asterisk are still in preparation and subject to changes in authorship should unforeseen circumstances prevent any author from completing his manuscript.

Published by
Glasgow, Brook & Company
at 15 Wilton Avenue
TORONTO, CANADA